THE BEST OF LODGE®

OUR 140 + MOST LOVED RECIPES

THE BEST OF LODGE®

OUR 140 + MOST LOVED RECIPES

Oxmoor House®

©2018 Lodge Manufacturing Company

Images ©2018 Time Inc. Books, a division of Meredith Corporation

Published by Oxmoor House, an imprint of Time Inc. Books
225 Liberty Street, New York, NY 10281

Assistant Editor: April Colburn
Project Editor: Lacie Pinyan
Design Director: Melissa Clark
Photo Director: Paden Reich
Designer: Teresa Cole
Photographers: Caroline Allison, Jim Bathie, Hélène Dujardin,
   Beau Gustafson, Art Meripol, Alison Miksch, Matt Niebuhr,
   Mary Britton Senseney
Prop Stylists: Cindy Barr, Mary Clayton Carl, Kay E. Clarke,
   Katherine Eckert Coyne, Missie Neville Crawford,
   Lydia DeGaris-Pursell, Mindi Shapiro Levine, Mary Louise Menendez
Food Stylists: Margaret Monroe Dickey, Tami Hardeman, Erica Hopper,
   Catherine Crowell Steele
Recipe Developers and Testers: Oxmoor House Test Kitchen,
   Kathleen Royal Phillips
Senior Production Manager: Greg A. Amason
Assistant Production and Project Manager: Kelsey Smith
Copy Editor: Adrienne Davis
Proofreader: Julie Gillis
Indexer: Mary Ann Laurens
Fellows: Holly Ravazzolo, Hanna Yokeley

ISBN-13: 978-0-8487-5794-6
Library of Congress Control Number: 2018949748

First Edition
Printed in the United States of America
10 9 8 7 6 5 4 3 2 1

We welcome your comments and suggestions about Time Inc. Books.
Time Inc. Books
Attention: Book Editors
P.O. Box 62310
Tampa, Florida 33662-2310

Time Inc. Books products may be purchased for business or promotional
use. For information on bulk purchases, please contact Christi Crowley
in the Special Sales Department at (845) 895-9858.

NOTE TO READER

The publisher of this book has made every reasonable effort to ensure that
the activities in this book are safe if conducted as instructed and performed
with reasonable skill and care. However, the publisher cannot and does not
assume any responsibility or liability whatsoever for any damage caused or
injury sustained while performing any of the activities contained in this book.
You are solely responsible for taking all reasonable and necessary safety
precautions when performing any of the activities contained in this book.

~ CONTENTS ~

❧ WELCOME ❧

There's something special about cookware passed down from generation to generation. The same skillets, Dutch ovens, and servers held in different hands create a bond that transcends time and space, connecting those who have known one another and even those who have not. Equally thrilling is being first in that chain to pass down cherished pieces, imagining in whose kitchen they will come to live. Under your care, once-new cast iron pieces can become hardworking heirlooms seasoned across a lifetime.

For a legacy like this, your cookware must be top quality, and for that, look no further than Lodge. The all-American, family-run-and-owned company has manufactured and gifted buyers with durable and reliable cast iron cookware since 1896. Day after day for decades, home cooks like you have used their Lodge pieces to make breakfast, lunch, and dinner because they know the products are built to last and make food taste delicious.

The recipes in this book are Lodge's picks for the best of the best. They're the most essential recipes to have in your repertoire for everything from hosting a holiday meal or dinner party to preparing simple weeknight meals. The selection showcases the best variety of flavors, ingredients, and dish types, offering recipes for breakfast, dessert, side dishes, and main-course meats, poultry, and seafood. With more than 140 recipes such as Sorghum French Toast (page 21), Chicken and Mushroom Stew with Wild Rice (page 62), Baked Spaghetti (page 115), and Simple Berry Skillet Cobbler (page 272), there are plenty of delicious options to choose from. Each recipe calls for time-tested Lodge cookware and has been contributed by Lodge-Kellermann family members, chefs, cooking instructors, food journalists, everyday home cooks, and other Lodge lovers. Anecdotes, cooking tips, and technique pointers from the contributors accompany the recipes throughout.

Our hope is that these recipes will become staples in your kitchen, that they will satisfy everyone at your table, and that you will share them with friends and pass them down through your family for generations—perhaps along with a well-loved piece of your very own Lodge cast iron.

Happy cooking,

The Editors

❧ THE LODGE CAST IRON LEGACY ❧

In 1896, Englishman Joseph Lodge selected the tiny town of South Pittsburg, Tennessee, to be home to his foundry, and today it continues to produce cast iron skillets, Dutch ovens, griddles, kettles, and grill pans. Cast iron pots and kettles became popular in the seventh and eighth centuries, with cooks the world over singing praises about their versatility and durability.

The primary quality that inspires the devotion of Lodge fans is the heat-seeking nature of cast iron, a fact known and appreciated by everyone from George Washington's mother, Mary Ball Washington, who valued her cast iron cookware so much that it's mentioned in her will; to Lewis and Clark, who brought the cookware with them on their expedition of discovery; to 21st-century cooks who use it to bake, sear, broil, sauté, fry, braise, and stir-fry meals on their stove-tops, in their ovens, and over campfires.

ASK ANY DEVOTEE OF LODGE ABOUT THEIR FAVORITE COOKWARE, AND YOU WILL HEAR A CONSTANT REFRAIN: "COOKWARE FADS MAY COME AND GO, BUT CAST IRON COOKWARE IS FOREVER."

Tennessee is known for many things: frontiersman Davy Crockett, the Jack Daniel's Distillery, Elvis Presley, and Nashville, America's Music City. As the sole domestic manufacturer of cast iron cookware and the oldest family-owned cookware company in the United States, Lodge shares the stage with many of the state's luminaries; however, the universal acclaim for its cast iron cookware and its historical connection with our nation's past arguably places Lodge at the soul of American cooking.

Throughout the 20th century, Lodge survived the development of numerous new metals for several enduring reasons: Cast iron is not only a superior conductor of heat, but it also heats slowly and evenly and retains heat longer than any other cookware. In addition, cast iron cookware resists scorching and burning, and it cooks food evenly—treasured attributes when frying or searing.

Not all cast iron cookware is created equal. In recent years, several brands of inferior imported cast iron cookware have entered the market. While the price might have initially been attractive, customers have come back

to Lodge, their enthusiasm for its cookware backed by the stringent quality control of the Lodge foundry. Maintaining foundry traditions established centuries earlier and using a privately held metal formula that was developed just for cookware, each piece of Lodge Cast Iron is created by pouring molten iron into individual sand molds. Lodge metal chemistry is monitored with every pour, a standard not found in any other cast iron foundry in the world. The exacting quality control produces cookware with legendary cooking performance that becomes better generation after generation.

The heritage of the Lodge family goes beyond its iconic cast iron cookware. Company founder Joseph Lodge had two children, Richard Lodge and Edith Lodge Kellermann, who each had children of their own. The fact that the Lodge-Kellermann family is one with exceptional cooks and masters of cast iron in their own kitchens isn't a surprise. Within these pages, you'll find recipes contributed by the Lodge-Kellermann family, as well as by their "extended family" of chefs, food writers, and exceptional home cooks, all of whom look to Lodge for the cookware and recipes they need to make memorable dishes.

BREAKFAST

These morning-time recipes, such as Sorghum
French Toast, Shirred Eggs with Ham and
Tomato, and Beef-Bacon Hash, make it easy
to wake up each morning and keep you
satisfied throughout the day.

Lynda King Kellermann shared with her mother, Eula Renfro King, a love for cooking for her family and carried on her mother's breakfast tradition by regularly making pancakes for her husband and children. In 1974, she added these Oatmeal Buttermilk Pancakes to her lineup after clipping the recipe from an issue of *Southern Living*.

OATMEAL BUTTERMILK PANCAKES

Makes 14 to 16 (3-inch) pancakes

- 2 cups quick-cooking oats
- ½ teaspoon baking soda
- 2½ cups buttermilk
- 1 cup all-purpose flour
- 2 tablespoons sugar
- 2 teaspoons baking powder
- 1 teaspoon salt
- ⅓ cup salad oil (such as canola, peanut, or light olive)
- 2 large eggs, beaten

1. In a large bowl, combine the oats, baking soda, and buttermilk. Let stand 5 minutes.

2. In a small bowl, combine the flour, sugar, baking powder, and salt. Add the flour mixture to the oat mixture along with the oil and eggs. Stir until blended.

3. Lightly grease a Lodge Reversible Pro-Grid Iron Griddle. Place over medium heat. Wait a few minutes, then fling a drop of water onto the griddle; if the water dances, the griddle's ready! For each pancake, pour about ¼ cup batter onto the griddle. Cook until golden brown on both sides, turning only once.

LODGE-KELLERMANN FAMILY MEMORIES

Whenever Lynda prepared pancakes, her husband, Charles Richard "Dick" Kellermann, Jr., grandson of company founder Joseph Lodge, would tell his children how his mother, Edith Kellermann, used pancakes to play a practical joke on her seven children. On April 1st, she would cut rounds of white flannel, dip them in the pancake batter, and cook them up like pancakes. Each child's serving included at least one of these "special" pancakes. When each child discovered the flannel cake, their mama would gleefully exclaim, "April Fool!"

If you want your pancake to be really full of fruit, use two apples (the sautéing will be a little awkward at first, but the slices eventually cook down), and adjust the amount of sugar and cinnamon to taste. Cookbook editor Pam Hoenig adapted the original recipe in *The Breakfast Book* by Marion Cunningham to make just a single serving for her daughter, Hannah.

HANNAH'S APPLE PANCAKE

Serves 1 generously

- ¼ cup (½ stick) unsalted butter
- ¼ cup milk
- 1 apple (Hannah prefers Golden Delicious)
- 2 tablespoons sugar
- ½ teaspoon ground cinnamon
- 1 large egg
- ¼ cup all-purpose flour
- Pinch of salt

1. Preheat the oven to 425°F. Melt the butter in a Lodge 5-inch cast iron skillet over low heat.

2. While the butter melts, pour the milk into a 2-cup measuring cup. Peel the apple, then cut it off the core into 4 pieces. Cut each piece lengthwise into thin slices. In a small bowl, toss the apple slices with the sugar and cinnamon until well coated.

3. Pour half the melted butter into the milk, and whisk well.

4. Add the apple slices and any loose sugar in the bowl to the hot butter in the skillet. Cook the apple slices over medium-low to low heat, turning them a few times, until softened; the sugar and butter will get nicely browned and bubbly. Remove the skillet from the heat.

5. Add the egg to the milk mixture, and whisk to combine. Add the flour and salt, and whisk until the batter is smooth. Pour the batter over the apples in the skillet, covering them.

6. Bake until the pancake puffs up and gets golden on top, with patches of brown, about 10 minutes. Enjoy the pancake straight from the skillet, or invert it onto a serving plate.

A CAST IRON MEMORY

When my mother-in-law, Constance Kingsley, passed away at the age of 88 and her household effects were being divided up, I made a beeline for her cast iron, which included 9- and 6½-inch skillets. I have fond memories of my father-in-law, George Kingsley, cooking bacon in the larger skillet when we came to visit, but I had never seen him use the smaller one. I soon discovered my own use for it—baking a single-serving German pancake, my daughter Hannah's favorite breakfast food. Her Mimi and Poppy would be delighted with its new use.

—Pam Hoenig

Sarah "Pat" Kirkwood Lodge married Rev. John Richard Lodge, grandson of company founder Joseph Lodge, five years after they met at Auburn University during World War II. She enjoyed good food and exchanged recipes with cooks in the parishes John served. Serve Aebleskiver with maple syrup, jam, jelly, or sprinkled with powdered sugar.

AEBLESKIVER

Makes 30 aebleskiver

4 large eggs, separated
2 cups cake flour
1 tablespoon sugar
1 teaspoon baking powder
½ teaspoon salt
¼ cup vegetable shortening, melted
Scant 2 cups milk (2 cups less 2 tablespoons)

1. In a large bowl, beat the egg yolks with an electric mixer until thick and pale. Wash and dry the beaters. In a medium bowl, beat the egg whites with the mixer until stiff peaks form.

2. In another medium bowl, sift together the flour, sugar, baking powder, and salt. Add the dry ingredients alternately with the melted shortening and milk to the beaten egg yolks. Lightly mix in the beaten egg whites with a whisk.

3. Heat a Lodge Aebleskiver pan over medium heat. Brush a small amount of shortening or oil in each well, and fill almost full with batter. Cook over medium heat until bubbly; using knitting needles, wooden skewers, or a small fondue fork, turn each one over after 30 seconds and continue to turn them every 30 seconds until all the sides are cooked to form a ball. Continue to turn them until browned on all sides. Remove from the pan.

4. Repeat with the remaining batter, then serve as you like.

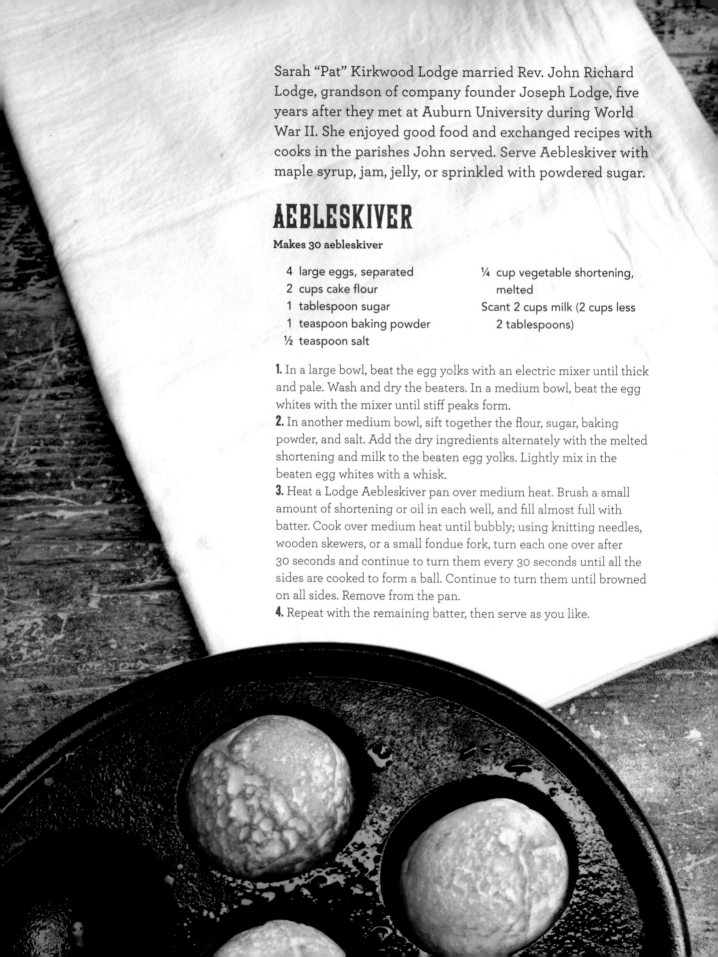

Crêpes were always a special treat when Connecticut-based marketing consultant and blogger (myMEGusta.com) Mary Ellen Griffin visited her grandparents. Originally from rural Quebec, her grandparents emigrated to New England. Her grandmother's crêpes weren't the lacy type you might find in Parisian bistros. They were hearty, making them perfect for breakfast on a cold winter morning. Serve topped with fresh blackberries and raspberries, if desired.

MEME'S FRENCH CANADIAN FARMHOUSE CRÊPES

Serves 1 (makes 2 crepes)

1 large egg
½ cup milk
⅓ cup all-purpose flour
Dash of salt

1 tablespoon lard
    or vegetable oil
Pure maple syrup

1. In a small bowl, whisk together the egg, milk, flour, and salt until the mixture is smooth.
2. Heat a Lodge 9-inch cast iron skillet over high heat. When the pan is VERY hot, add the lard, and swirl to coat the pan with it. Pour in half the crêpe mixture (about 3 ounces), and swirl the pan to coat the bottom with the batter. The crêpe will cook quickly, in less than a minute per side. Using a fork and knife, as soon as the batter starts to solidify, lift the crêpe up, and rotate it to ensure even browning. Once browned, flip the crêpe. Rotate it in the same way; when evenly browned, remove it to a warm plate, stacking between sheets of wax paper to prevent sticking, and repeat with the remaining crêpe batter.
3. Serve immediately with the maple syrup.

Ninth-generation Southerner Rebecca Lang lives in Athens, Georgia, and is a cooking instructor and author. Her fancy version of French toast is as comforting and rich as it is beautiful. Right out of the oven, it's puffed high above the skillet edge, calling for a memorable morning around the table.

SORGHUM FRENCH TOAST

Serves 6 to 8

- ¼ cup (½ stick) unsalted butter, cut into 8 pieces, plus ½ tablespoon unsalted butter
- 10 ounces challah bread
- 1¼ cups whole milk
- ¾ cup heavy cream
- 8 large eggs
- ¼ cup sorghum syrup (see Kitchen Note)
- ⅓ cup granulated sugar
- 2 tablespoons vanilla extract
- ⅛ teaspoon salt
- ½ teaspoon ground cinnamon
- ⅛ teaspoon ground allspice
- ⅛ teaspoon ground nutmeg
- ⅛ teaspoon ground ginger
- 2 teaspoons confectioners' sugar

1. Grease a Lodge 9-inch cast iron skillet with the ½ tablespoon of the butter.

2. Cut the bread into 1-inch-thick slices. Cut each slice into 6 pieces. Arrange in the skillet in a single layer, crust sides up.

3. In a large bowl, whisk together the milk, cream, eggs, sorghum syrup, granulated sugar, vanilla, and salt. Pour evenly over the bread. Refrigerate for 45 minutes.

4. Remove the skillet from the refrigerator, and let sit at room temperature for 20 minutes. Preheat the oven to 350°F.

5. In a small bowl, combine the spices. Sprinkle over the bread. Arrange the pieces of butter evenly over the top. Bake until puffed and golden brown, about 45 minutes.

6. Remove from the oven. Use a small sieve or tea strainer to dust the confectioners' sugar over the top. Serve immediately, straight from the skillet.

KITCHEN NOTE:
Sorghum syrup pours like honey and tastes milder than molasses. The coveted dark golden syrup can be found at Southern roadside stands and upscale grocery stores. If you can't find it, use maple syrup.

A COOKING SECRET FROM REBECCA

Don't be tempted to skimp on the bread-and-egg-mixture soaking time. To achieve this dish's signature soft, creamy center, you'll want to give the mixture at least 45 minutes to penetrate the bread.

This cake is velvety, tender, and buttery, and the crumbs are big, dense, and sweet. It's an over-the-top rendition in the style David Bowers prefers in his cookbook *Bake It Like a Man: A Real Man's Cookbook*. With a layer of ripe peach slices (or plum, if you prefer) between the cake and topping, this is a real bakery-style coffee cake—the kind that makes you glad to face the morning. Served slightly warm with a scoop of vanilla ice cream, it also makes a fine dessert. For best results, remove any leftover cake from the skillet before storing.

FRESH PEACH CRUMB COFFEE CAKE

Serves 8

TOPPING

- 1½ cups all-purpose flour
- ½ cup firmly packed light brown sugar
- ½ cup granulated sugar
- 1½ teaspoons ground cinnamon
- ½ cup (1 stick) salted butter, melted

CAKE BATTER

- ½ cup (1 stick) salted butter, softened
- ½ cup granulated sugar
- ½ cup sour cream
- 2 large eggs
- 1½ teaspoons vanilla extract
- 1¼ cups all-purpose flour
- ½ teaspoon baking soda
- ½ teaspoon baking powder
- 1 pound ripe peaches (3 to 4 medium), peeled, pitted, and sliced

1. Prepare the Topping: Preheat the oven to 350°F. Liberally butter the bottom of a Lodge 10-inch cast iron skillet.

2. Place all the ingredients in a medium bowl, and mix well to make a dense, smooth dough; set aside.

3. Prepare the Cake Batter: Cream the butter and granulated sugar in a large bowl with an electric mixer until smooth. Add the sour cream, eggs, and vanilla, and beat well. Place the flour, baking soda, and baking powder in a small bowl, stirring to combine; add to the batter all at once, stirring well to combine. The batter will be stiff.

4. Smooth the batter into the prepared skillet. Arrange the peach slices on top in a single layer. Crumble the topping mixture into big chunks, and sprinkle on top of the peaches.

5. Bake until a toothpick inserted in the center comes out with crumbs clinging to it, about 45 minutes. (The cake will remain quite moist because of the peaches, but be sure you don't have streaks of raw batter on the toothpick.) Cool a little before cutting into wedges.

Sarah "Pat" Kirkwood Lodge, who was married to company founder Joseph Lodge's grandson, Rev. John Richard Lodge, often made quick breads like Bran Muffins to serve for breakfast and at afternoon tea or to give to new neighbors. It is believed that this recipe came from the Hemlock Inn in North Carolina, one of Pat and John's favorite places to visit.

BRAN MUFFINS

Makes 36 muffins

6 cups All-Bran cereal
2 cups boiling water
1 cup (2 sticks) salted butter, melted
2 cups sugar
4 large eggs, beaten

1 quart buttermilk
5 cups bleached all-purpose flour
5 teaspoons baking soda
2 teaspoons salt

1. Preheat the oven to 425°F. Place 2 cups of the cereal in a large bowl. Pour the boiling water over the cereal, and let stand a few minutes. Mix in the melted butter, sugar, eggs, buttermilk, and the remaining 4 cups cereal.

2. In another large bowl, sift the flour, baking soda, and salt together. Add to the cereal mixture, mixing thoroughly.

3. Spoon the batter into a well-greased Lodge (6-cup) cast iron muffin pan, filling each well to just below the top. Bake until a wooden pick inserted in the center of the muffins comes out clean, about 15 to 20 minutes. Repeat using the remaining batter.

KITCHEN NOTE:

The batter can be stored in an airtight container and refrigerated up to 1 week. The batter is good to go as soon as it is mixed.

These muffins from Martha Holland, who writes a weekly cooking column for her local paper, freeze very nicely. Let them cool completely, then freeze them in zip-top plastic freezer bags. To reheat, let the muffins thaw for about 15 minutes, wrap them tightly in aluminum foil, and place them in a preheated 400°F oven for 15 minutes.

HAM AND SAUSAGE MUFFINS

Makes 12 muffins

1 tablespoon butter
¼ cup finely chopped green bell pepper
¼ cup finely chopped green onions
½ cup plus 2 tablespoons all-purpose flour
½ cup yellow cornmeal
½ teaspoon baking soda
½ teaspoon salt
1 large egg
¾ cup buttermilk
⅓ cup finely chopped ham
⅓ cup finely chopped cooked sausage

1. Preheat the oven to 400°F. Grease two Lodge (6-cup) cast iron muffin pans.
2. In a small Lodge cast iron skillet, melt the butter, and cook the bell pepper and green onions over medium heat until softened but not browned, stirring constantly.
3. In a large bowl, sift together the flour, cornmeal, baking soda, and salt. In a medium bowl, beat the egg, then stir in the buttermilk. Add the egg mixture to the flour mixture all at once, stirring only until blended; do not overstir. Carefully fold in the ham, sausage, and bell pepper mixture, along with any butter left in the skillet.
4. Spoon the batter into the prepared muffin pans, filling each well full. Bake until nicely browned, about 20 minutes. Cool in the pans 5 minutes. Remove the muffins from the pans, and cool completely on a wire rack.

Marco Fossati, former executive chef of Quattro, located at the Four Seasons in Palo Alto, California, was inspired to add his favorite childhood dish to the brunch menu. Simply called Tomato and Egg, it was known to rouse Marco from bed on Saturday mornings and send him bounding into the kitchen. Featuring fresh organic eggs (purchased from the family-run cage-free Glaum Egg Ranch) roasted in a cast iron skillet, this dish quickly became a hotel favorite, too.

TOMATO AND EGG

Serves 4

- 3 cups Salsa di Pelati (recipe follows)
- 8 large organic eggs
- 8 thin slices Tuscan-style country bread, toasted
- 3 tablespoons freshly grated Parmigiano-Reggiano cheese
- 1 tablespoon fresh basil leaves
- Freshly ground black pepper
- Tuscan extra virgin olive oil for drizzling

1. Preheat the oven to 325°F.

2. Divide the marinara between two Lodge 10-inch cast iron skillets, and bring to a simmer over medium heat. Reduce the heat to low, and crack 4 eggs into the sauce in each skillet. Place the skillets in the oven, and bake until the egg whites are opaque but the yolks are still soft, 7 to 9 minutes.

3. For each serving, place 2 slices of the toasted bread in a large shallow soup bowl or Lodge cast iron round mini server. Spoon the marinara and 2 eggs onto each piece of toast. Sprinkle each evenly with the cheese, basil, and freshly ground black pepper; drizzle with a little oil.

SALSA DI PELATI (MARINARA)

Makes about 6 cups

- 2 medium yellow onions, finely chopped
- 3 garlic cloves, sliced
- ¼ cup olive oil
- 2 (28-ounce) cans peeled whole San Marzano tomatoes, undrained, chopped
- 16 fresh basil leaves

1. In a Lodge 5-quart cast iron Dutch oven, cook the onions and garlic in the oil over medium heat until translucent, about 5 minutes.

2. Stir in the tomatoes, and simmer, uncovered, for about 1½ hours, adjusting the heat to prevent scorching and stirring occasionally.

3. Turn the heat off, and stir in the basil. Let steep as the sauce cools completely. Remove the basil before using.

This recipe, suitable for breakfast or a light lunch, is from chef David Waltuck. Now the director of culinary affairs and chef instructor at the Institute of Culinary Education in New York City, Waltuck is also known for the innovative and elegant cuisine served at Chanterelle, his groundbreaking former restaurant in downtown NYC. Not as well known is the brief period when Chanterelle experimented with breakfast service. Simple yet luxurious, this dish epitomizes the Chanterelle approach. It makes one serving, so multiply amounts for additional servings as desired. You'll need a mini 5-inch cast iron skillet for each serving.

SHIRRED EGGS WITH HAM AND TOMATO

Serves 1; recipe may be multiplied

- 1 tablespoon unsalted butter
- 2 slices Black Forest or other cooked ham, trimmed to fit pan
- 2 tablespoons tomato sauce, homemade or good-quality jarred
- 2 extra-large eggs
- 1 tablespoon heavy cream
- Salt and freshly ground black pepper
- 1 teaspoon coarsely chopped fresh herbs (tarragon, chervil, and/or chives—just one herb or a mixture)

1. Preheat the oven to 350°F.

2. Melt the butter in a Lodge 5-inch cast iron skillet over low heat. Remove the skillet from the heat.

3. Place the ham in the bottom of the pan. Spread the tomato sauce evenly over the ham. Carefully break the eggs on top; drizzle the cream over the eggs. Season with the salt and pepper to taste (go very light on the salt since the ham is salty).

4. Place the pan in the oven, and bake for 5 to 6 minutes, checking occasionally. The whites should be set; the yolks can still be runny.

5. Sprinkle the eggs with the herbs, and serve in the skillet.

CHILAQUILES WITH FRIED EGGS AND TOMATILLO SALSA

Serves 6

"One of my favorite breakfast memories as a kid growing up in Minneapolis was my dad serving me blood sausage. He served the Russian-style kind with buckwheat in it. He cut it on an angle and slowly sautéed it in a Lodge cast iron pan until it was crispy on both cut sides and tender and hot inside," remembers Cindy Pawlcyn, Napa Valley-based chef/restaurateur, caterer, and cookbook author. Cindy's all-time favorite breakfast is the corn tortilla casserole, chilaquiles. It's perfect for brunch, as it will hold well in a warm oven, and both the salsa and corn chips can be made ahead. "My garden has more tomatillos than tomatoes, so I always do a green tomatillo version," she says, but you can easily substitute red tomatoes.

CHILAQUILES

2 to 3 tablespoons peanut or vegetable oil

12 (6-inch) corn tortillas, each cut into 6 wedges

1 recipe Tomatillo Salsa (recipe at right)

½ cup grated queso fresco or a high-moisture Monterey Jack cheese

½ cup goat cheese, separated into small pieces

1 to 2 tablespoons unsalted butter or nonstick cooking spray

6 large eggs, preferably farm-fresh

Kosher salt and freshly ground black pepper to taste

GARNISHES

6 to 12 tablespoons crumbled goat cheese

12 small sprigs fresh cilantro

12 tablespoons crème fraîche

6 slices ripe avocado

6 lime wedges (optional)

1. Prepare the Chilaquiles: Heat the oil in a Lodge 10- or 12-inch cast iron skillet over medium-high heat. When the oil is almost smoking, add the tortillas, breaking them apart, and cook, stirring, until crispy. Drain any excess oil from the skillet, then pour the Tomatillo Salsa over the tortillas, and mix well. Add the queso fresco and ½ cup goat cheese, and mix lightly. Reduce the heat to low.

2. Heat a Lodge 12-inch cast iron griddle over medium-low heat. Heat 6 serving plates in a warm oven.

3. Melt the butter over the surface of the griddle, or remove from the heat, and coat with cooking spray. Gently break the eggs onto the griddle, trying to keep them separate from one another. Cook them sunny side up, and season with the salt and pepper to taste. Just before the eggs finish cooking, stir the chilaquiles, and place a portion of the mixture in the center of each warm plate. Top each serving with a fried egg.

4. Prepare the Garnishes: Sprinkle each serving with 1 to 2 tablespoons of the goat cheese, and tuck in 2 of the cilantro sprigs. Drizzle each with 2 tablespoons of the crème fraîche, and top with a slice of the avocado. Serve a lime wedge on the side, if desired.

TOMATILLO SALSA

Makes 4½ to 5 cups

- 4 cups tomatillos, peeled from their papery husks
- 4 garlic cloves, peeled
- ½ medium onion, roughly chopped
- 3 serrano chiles
- 1 cup water
- ¼ to ½ teaspoon kosher salt, to taste
- 2 tablespoons peanut or vegetable oil

In a blender, puree the tomatillos, garlic, onion, chiles, water, and salt until smooth. Heat the oil in a Lodge 10-inch cast iron skillet over medium-high heat for about 2 minutes; add the puree—it will splatter, so be careful. Cook until heated through, 3 to 4 minutes. Keep warm until needed.

"Our cast iron skillet is particularly special to my husband, Mark, and me because close friends gave it to us as a wedding gift. We use it all the time, and in the years we've been married, it has taken on that lovely seasoned quality that we know will just get better and better—kind of like our relationship!" says Beth Lipton, former food director of *Health* and *All You* magazines. "Weekend breakfasts are a big deal at our house, and we always grab the cast iron skillet when making hearty frittatas like this one."

SMOKED SALMON AND SCALLION FRITTATA

Serves 4 to 6

- 4 scallions or green onions, trimmed
- 2 tablespoons olive oil
- 1 medium sweet onion, such as Vidalia, roughly chopped
- Salt and freshly ground black pepper
- 8 large eggs
- ½ cup whole milk
- 4 ounces smoked salmon (see Kitchen Note), chopped
- 1 (3-ounce) package cream cheese, softened, pulled into pieces

1. Preheat the oven to 375°F.

2. Roughly chop the white and light green parts of the scallions. If desired, slice the dark green parts of 2 scallions, and set aside for garnish.

3. Warm the oil in a Lodge 10-inch cast iron skillet over medium-high heat. Add the onion and white and light green parts of the scallions, sprinkle lightly with the salt, and season generously with the pepper. Cook, stirring occasionally, until just tender, 3 to 5 minutes.

4. In a large bowl, whisk together the eggs and milk until well blended. Pour into the skillet. Scatter the salmon pieces and bits of cream cheese all over the top of the frittata. Season with more pepper, if desired. Cook the frittata on the stove without stirring for 3 minutes, then transfer the skillet to the oven. Bake until the frittata is nearly set in the center, about 10 minutes.

5. Turn the oven to low broil, and cook until the frittata is just set in the center, 1 to 2 minutes longer.

6. Remove the skillet from the oven, and let stand for 5 minutes. Sprinkle with the reserved scallion greens, if desired; cut into wedges, and serve.

KITCHEN NOTE:
Buy the most flavorful smoked salmon you can get. Beth likes the wild sockeye salmon from Trader Joe's. Snipped chives or a light sprinkling of fresh dill would make a pretty garnish instead of the scallions.

This recipe from Amy Beth Edelman, chef and co-owner of The Night Kitchen Bakery in Philadelphia, is perfect for a holiday brunch or served to guests as a light lunch.

SPINACH, TOMATO, AND BACON FRITTATA

Serves 6 to 8

1 pound sliced bacon
4 ounces fresh baby spinach
¼ cup halved cherry tomatoes
15 medium eggs
1 tablespoon kosher salt

1 teaspoon freshly ground black pepper
2 cups (8 ounces) grated white Cheddar cheese

1. Preheat the oven to 350°F.

2. In a deep Lodge 12-inch cast iron skillet, fry the bacon over medium-high heat until crisp (you may need to do this in several batches). Remove to paper towels to drain.

3. Pour all the bacon fat out of the skillet except for 1 tablespoon. Add the spinach and tomatoes, and cook over medium heat, stirring a few times, until the spinach wilts and the tomatoes heat through.

4. In a large bowl, scramble the eggs, and season with the salt and pepper. Pour into the skillet over the spinach and tomatoes. Evenly sprinkle the cheese over the top. Crumble the bacon, and sprinkle over the cheese.

5. Bake until the center is set, 25 to 30 minutes. Let rest on top of the stove for 10 minutes before cutting into wedges to serve.

How Amy Beth Makes a Frittata

1. For the best flavor, build depth and dimension during each cooking step. Start by browning bacon and reserving the browned bits. Sauté the aromatic spinach and tomatoes in the bacon grease to intensify their flavors and to dissolve the browned bits in the pan.

2. Add salt and pepper to the eggs after the eggs have been beaten with a whisk. This step guarantees that the seasoning will be evenly dispersed.

3. For an added hit of flavor, use just one skillet, and pour the egg mixture over the spinach and tomatoes. Sprinkle with crumbled bacon and cheese.

4. After baking, let the frittata rest on top of the stove or a nearby surface for 10 minutes to let the eggs set and the flavors meld.

When California-based food historian and author Betty Fussell wants to make hash, she uses cast iron. Once it gets hot, it stays hot. And, of course, cast iron provides the perfect nonstick surface. Once seasoned, it stays seasoned. "Unless, of course," Betty says, "you ruin it with soap and water, but I don't know anyone foolish enough to do that."

BEEF-BACON HASH

Serves 4

- 3 slices bacon
- ½ cup finely chopped onion
- 2 cups new potatoes, cut into ½-inch cubes and parboiled 5 minutes
- 1 cup cubed (½-inch) leftover cooked beef or other meat
- 2 garlic cloves, minced
- 1 tablespoon fresh thyme leaves or ½ teaspoon dried
- Sea salt and freshly ground black pepper (Betty likes to add a lot of pepper)
- ¼ cup (or more) fresh flat-leaf parsley leaves, chopped

1. In a Lodge cast iron skillet (preferably 10 inches in diameter or more) over medium heat, fry the bacon until crisp. Remove the bacon to a paper towel to drain, and pour off all but a thin layer of fat.
2. Add the onion to the skillet, and cook for 2 to 3 minutes over medium heat, stirring.
3. Increase the heat to medium-high, and add the potatoes to the onions in a single layer (you may need to brown the potatoes in two batches, depending on the size of the skillet). Cook until the potatoes are browned on both sides, about 5 minutes.
4. Add the beef, and lower the heat slightly. Add the garlic and thyme, season with the salt and pepper to taste, mix well, and heat thoroughly.
5. Remove the pan from the heat, and add the parsley. Crumble the bacon (or cut into small pieces), and add to the hash. Mix well, and serve hot or at room temperature.

A CAST IRON MEMORY

My Grandma Harper used two cast iron skillets all her life, until she gave them to me when I got married. That was over 60 years ago, so the skillets must be well over a century old. I recently gave the larger one to cookbook author Grace Young, also known as "The Wok Queen." I kept the smaller one.

Both skillets had traveled with Grandma from Nebraska to Colorado to Southern California, where she and Grandpa raised me. Back then, she made beef hash pretty much the way I make it now, except when I was a kid the beef she used came out of a can.

The chief virtue of hash is that it's thrifty. I use steak, but leftover meats of any kind will do, particularly those you don't want to overcook but just mix and crisp up. Kicking it off with bacon adds magic flavor and texture. Grandma Harper was not looking for such niceties. Thrift was her god. She always had a can of saved bacon fat near her stove, ready for whatever she decided to fry in her skillets. And so do I.

—Betty Fussell

Stuffed tomatoes are hearty and satisfying, like a whole meal unto themselves. Minneapolis-based lifestyle expert Ross Sveback wanted to come up with a rendition for breakfast. "I immediately knew maple syrup had to be in it, along with sage, and the rest was easy." Ross serves these in individual Lodge 6½-inch cast iron skillets alongside poached eggs.

SAUSAGE AND MAPLE STUFFED TOMATOES

Serves 6 to 8

6 to 8 ripe medium tomatoes
Kosher salt
1 pound bulk country-blend pork sausage (don't use Italian seasoned)
1 medium onion, cut into ½-inch pieces
4 garlic cloves, minced
7 to 8 ounces button mushrooms, cut into ½-inch pieces

2 tablespoons olive oil
½ cup pure maple syrup (Ross likes to use Burton's Maplewood Farm)
2 cups plain dry breadcrumbs
2 tablespoons chopped fresh sage
1 cup (4 ounces) grated Parmesan cheese
Coarsely ground black pepper to taste

1. Core the tomatoes and, using a melon baller, scoop out the insides. Sprinkle the salt on the inside of each tomato, and set upside down for 30 minutes on a wire rack set over the sink or a baking sheet to catch the juice.

2. While the tomatoes drain, cook the sausage in a Lodge 12-inch cast iron skillet over medium heat until no longer pink, breaking it into small pieces. Using a slotted spoon, transfer it to paper towels. Do not drain the fat from the pan. Add the onion and garlic, and cook, stirring a few times, until translucent, 4 to 5 minutes. Add the mushrooms and oil, and cook, stirring occasionally, until the mushrooms have released their moisture, about 10 minutes.

3. In a medium bowl, combine the sausage and mushroom mixture. Add the maple syrup, breadcrumbs, sage, cheese, and salt and pepper to taste.

4. Using your hands, evenly divide the filling among the tomatoes, gently pushing the filling in to pack it, and press a roughly ¼-cup mound on top of each tomato. Place the stuffed tomatoes on a baking sheet. At this point, you can cover the tomatoes with plastic wrap and refrigerate until ready to bake or overnight.

5. If you have refrigerated the tomatoes, remove them 30 minutes before you intend to bake them to take the chill off. Preheat the oven to 375°F. Replace the plastic wrap with aluminum foil, and bake, covered, for 30 minutes. Remove the foil, and bake for an additional 10 to 15 minutes. Serve immediately.

A COOKING SECRET FROM ROSS

Keeping the tomatoes covered two-thirds of the way through and then uncovering lets them steam-cook and not get overly browned and tough on top.

This recipe comes by way of Nancy Newsom Mahaffey, from Princeton, Kentucky. For a milder or less salty taste, Nancy recommends soaking the sliced ham in lukewarm water or sweet milk for up to 30 minutes before frying.

FRIED KENTUCKY COUNTRY HAM WITH NEWSOM FAMILY RED-EYE GRAVY

Serves 2 to 4

- 2 center slices (about ¼ inch thick) or 4 smaller boneless slices country ham
- ¾ cup hot brewed coffee
- 1 teaspoon brown sugar

1. To fry the ham, trim off the hard outer edge of the ham, and remove the rind. DO NOT TRIM THE FAT. This adds flavor, and no other fat will be needed for cooking.

2. Place the ham in a Lodge 12-inch cast iron skillet, turning the lean part away from what will be the hottest point of the skillet. Add just enough water to cover the bottom of the pan. Let the water evaporate over medium-low heat, then fry the ham slowly over medium to low heat. Do not overfry, as this will make the ham hard, dry, and tough. Turn the slices often. Country ham is usually done when the fat is transparent and beginning to brown. If you'd like to brown the ham just before taking it out of the pan, turn up the heat as necessary and very quickly turn the ham to brown it as you prefer. Remove the ham to serving plates.

3. To make the gravy, pour the pan drippings into a small bowl (see Kitchen Note). Return the skillet to medium heat. When the skillet is hot, pour in the coffee, stirring the sides and bottom of the skillet to loosen all the browned bits from frying the ham. Stir into the coffee, and cook for 3 to 5 minutes, maintaining just enough heat for the coffee to bubble. Add the brown sugar, and stir in well.

4. Pour the coffee into the center of the bowl with the drippings. Do not stir. You will see a "red eye" in the center of the bowl. (That's where the term "red-eye" gravy comes from.) Serve the gravy on the side.

KITCHEN NOTE:

If you end up with less than 2 tablespoons of drippings, the next time you want to make red-eye gravy, cook some extra fat or skins along with the slices. Nancy says that old-timers will tell you that young hams (less than 10 months old) do not make red-eye gravy.

 ## HAND-CRAFTED HAM

Nancy Newsom Mahaffey

Artisan ham maker and store owner, Princeton, Kentucky

Nancy Newsom Mahaffey, also known as "The Ham Lady," is the third-generation owner of Newsom's Old Mill Store and Colonel Bill Newsom's Aged Kentucky Country Ham. Nancy's grandfather, H.C. (Hosea Cleveland) Newsom, opened the mill store in 1917. "My father, Colonel Bill Newsom, who always wanted to be known simply as 'Bill,' used this recipe for country ham and red-eye gravy since at least the 1930s. I'm sure he must have learned it from his father and mother—H.C. and Ora Lee Newsom—for in my grandparents' day and in my dad's day, the days of the Great Depression, nothing was ever wasted," recalls Nancy. "I'm sure that the recipe for red-eye gravy was developed during the early days of my family, previous to 1900."

Newsom country hams continue an unbroken chain of curing tradition, dating back to the landing of a Newsom forefather in Jamestown, Virginia, in the 1640s. It is their mission to continue the preservation of the lost art of artisanal ham curing—an ambient weather cure that requires time and know-how. Newsom country hams are rubbed with salt and brown sugar (no nitrates permitted), hand washed, then hung to smoke over hickory wood. Several years ago, one of their hams was placed in a museum in Aracena, Spain, as part of the Fifth World Congress of Dry Cured Hams.

MY FATHER'S GRILLADES

Serves 8

- 2 pounds pork loin, clean of all fat and silverskin
- Kosher salt and freshly ground black pepper
- Sodium-free Creole or Cajun seasoning
- 3 cups all-purpose flour
- 1 cup canola oil
- 1½ cups (3 sticks) unsalted butter
- 2 large onions, finely chopped
- 2 large green bell peppers, seeded and finely chopped
- 3 celery ribs, finely chopped
- 2½ tablespoons minced garlic
- 2 large ripe tomatoes, diced
- 2 tablespoons chopped fresh thyme
- 3 quarts beef stock (if not homemade, use reduced-sodium organic)
- 2 tablespoons Worcestershire sauce
- 1 bay leaf

1. Slice the pork into very thin medallions (almost scaloppine). Vigorously season with the salt, pepper, and Creole seasoning on both sides. Lightly season the flour with the same three seasonings, and dredge the pork in it, tapping off any excess.

2. Heat the oil in a Lodge 15-inch cast iron skillet over medium heat. Dip the corner of one of the dredged pork medallions in the oil; if it begins to "fry," then the oil is ready; if it doesn't, wait until it does. When the oil is hot, sear the medallions in batches until nicely browned on both sides; don't crowd the pan. As the pork is browned, transfer it to a plate.

3. Drain the oil from the skillet (don't wipe the skillet clean). Heat the pan over medium-low heat, and add the butter. When the butter is melted, add 2 cups of the seasoned dredging flour, and stir with a wooden spoon to make a dark roux. Do not try to rush through this; if you take your time, your guests will be able to tell (if you don't, they'll know that as well). Slowly cook the roux, stirring every minute or two and scraping all the edges (never walk away from the pot).

4. Once the roux has taken on the color of semi dark chocolate (after about 1 hour), add the onions, bell peppers, and celery (collectively referred to as "the trinity" in South Louisiana). Cook your trinity, stirring, until the vegetables are tender. Add the garlic, tomatoes, and thyme, and cook, stirring, until aromatic. Whisk in the stock, and add the Worcestershire and bay leaf. Season to taste with the salt, pepper, and Creole seasoning. Bring to a simmer, and add the seared pork.

5. Preheat the oven to 250°F. Cover the skillet (with aluminum foil if you don't have a lid), and bake until the pork is tender, 1 to 1½ hours.

"This dish, more than any other, takes me back to my childhood," says Kelly English, chef-owner of Restaurant Iris and The Second Line in Memphis. "My dad would make the family a Dutch oven full of grillades that we would eat on all Sunday. It has appeared on our brunch menu at Restaurant Iris." Serve these grillades over stone-ground grits and with poached eggs.

❧ SOUPS, STEWS & CHILI ❧

There's something about a bowl of hot meat, vegetables, legumes, and more that comforts like nothing else. Dig into these dishes such as Winter Vegetable Chili, Chicken and Mushroom Stew with Wild Rice, and North Carolina Down East Clam Chowder on a cold day or any time you need a pick-me-up.

This recipe contributed by Cathy Black comes from her sister, Tammy Lee of Madisonville, Tennessee. Tammy's husband's aunt, Cathy Lee Plenge, gave Tammy the recipe. Aunt Cathy lives in Phoenix, Arizona, and has a huge garden with lots of zucchini, so she has many zucchini recipes. This is Tammy's favorite soup recipe. She can't wait for the zucchini crop to come in each summer so she can make it.

ZUCCHINI SOUP

Serves 4 to 6

6 small zucchini, trimmed and shredded
Salt
1 tablespoon olive oil
2 tablespoons salted butter
2 medium onions, finely minced
1 garlic clove, minced

5 cups chicken stock or broth
2 tablespoons chopped fresh herbs of your choice (oregano, basil, parsley, and/or chives)
2 tablespoons fresh lemon juice
Freshly ground black pepper

1. Place the shredded zucchini in a colander over a bowl, sprinkle with the salt, and allow to drain for about 30 minutes.

2. Heat the oil and butter together in a Lodge 5-quart cast iron Dutch oven over medium heat until the butter melts. Add the onions and garlic, and cook, stirring a few times, until the onions are golden, about 10 minutes.

3. Dry the zucchini on paper towels, and add to the onion mixture. Cook over low heat for about 5 minutes. Add the stock, and simmer for 15 minutes.

4. Using an immersion blender, puree the soup in the pot. Let the soup cool a little. Stir in the herbs and lemon juice, and season with the salt and pepper to taste. Reheat and serve.

❧ MY CAST IRON REDISCOVERY ❧

Sheri Castle

Author of The Southern Living Community Cookbook *and more,*
Chapel Hill, North Carolina

My family always cooked with cast iron, so I have no clear moment of discovery. However, my moment of rediscovery was when I got serious about cooking and started working hard at it. The first dish I prepared in cast iron was eggs. We had a little skillet that was just right for one or two eggs. I started with scrambled, moved on to fried, and eventually tackled omelets. No one in my family had ever even heard of an omelet until I made one for them. Shortly after, I learned that my cast iron pieces delivered more than memories. For some tasks, they outperformed my fancier, shinier, costlier pots and pans. Plus, they were reliable, durable, and tolerant of my ways.

Cast iron skillets were a given in my family's kitchens, as certain and commonplace as knives and bowls and aprons. For something to be considered an heirloom, some sort of sentiment must develop. That happened for me when a beloved aunt died unexpectedly more than 30 years ago. I inherited her engagement ring and some of her cast iron cookware. The ring is in a safe-deposit box, where I rarely see it. But the pans are in my kitchen cabinets, where I use them almost daily. I've also accumulated other family cast iron pieces, bought and refurbished old pieces from yard sales and flea markets, and invested in a few new items. My collection has grown to around 60 pieces. My favorite is a 9-inch skillet that was handed down from my great-grandmother. To my knowledge, for upwards of a century, nothing other than cornbread has ever been cooked in that one. It shines like ebony. Someday I will hand it down to my daughter. Until then, I use it to make my version of cornbread, which is my favorite cast iron recipe. It's sugar free, bacon blessed, and skillet born. It is the plain truth that cornbread must be made in a cast iron skillet.

"It is challenging to find a crowd-pleasing chili that features vegetables, but this one fits the bill. It's hearty, colorful, and full of flavor," says cookbook author Sheri Castle.

WINTER VEGETABLE CHILI

Serves 8

- 3 tablespoons vegetable oil
- 1 medium onion, chopped
- 2 medium garlic cloves, very finely chopped
- 2 large red, yellow, and/or orange bell peppers, seeded and cut into ½-inch pieces
- 4 small parsnips, peeled and cut into ½-inch pieces
- 2 large carrots, peeled and cut into ½-inch pieces
- 1 medium sweet potato or 1 small winter squash, peeled and cut into ½-inch pieces
- 1 teaspoon kosher salt, plus more to taste
- 2 tablespoons ground ancho or chipotle chile powder

- 1 tablespoon ground cumin
- 1 tablespoon ground coriander
- 1 teaspoon ground cinnamon
- 1 tablespoon smoked paprika
- 1 cup amber ale
- 1½ cups vegetable juice, such as V8
- 1 (14-ounce) can fire-roasted diced tomatoes, undrained
- 1 (15-ounce) can hominy, rinsed and drained
- 2 (15-ounce) cans black beans, rinsed and drained
- Orange wedges, sour cream, and corn chips, for serving

1. Heat the oil in a Lodge 3-quart enameled cast iron Dutch oven over medium-high heat. Add the onion, and cook, stirring often, until softened, about 5 minutes. Add the garlic, bell peppers, parsnips, carrots, sweet potato, and salt, and cook, stirring often, until the vegetables begin to soften, about 8 minutes.

2. Add the ground chile, cumin, coriander, cinnamon, and paprika, and cook, stirring constantly, for 3 minutes. Reduce the heat if the spices begin to scorch.

3. Add the ale and vegetable juice. Stir to scrape up the browned glaze from the bottom of the pot. Bring to a boil, reduce the heat, partially cover the pot, and simmer until the vegetables are almost tender, about 8 minutes, stirring occasionally.

4. Stir in the tomatoes, hominy, and beans. Simmer until heated through, about 8 minutes.

5. Season with the salt to taste. Serve warm with the oranges, sour cream, and chips on the side.

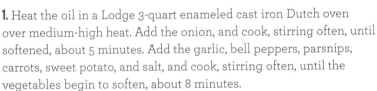

A COOKING SECRET FROM SHERI

For best results, make this chili at least one day ahead. To store, cool, cover, and refrigerate for up to 3 days. Warm over medium heat, and check the seasoning before serving.

The key to making this stew, says Massachusetts-based cookbook author and barbecue expert Mike Stines, is to do all the prep work ahead of time and have everything ready when it's needed. "If you dice the meat and vegetables into bite-size pieces," declares Mike, "you shouldn't need a knife for the stew." This stew, like any stew or chili, is better after standing for a day, but even without a nap in the fridge, it's tasty.

BEEF STEW WITH HERBED DUMPLINGS

Serves 6

BEEF STEW

- 2 tablespoons vegetable shortening
- 1½ pounds beef chuck, trimmed of fat and cut into ¾-inch cubes (about 1 pound trimmed)
- 1 pound beef top round, trimmed of fat and cut into ¾-inch cubes
- 1 tablespoon smoked paprika
- Coarse kosher salt and freshly ground black pepper
- 1½ teaspoons finely minced garlic
- ¼ cup tomato paste
- ¼ cup dark roux, plus more as needed
- 4 bay leaves
- 1 teaspoon dried rosemary, crushed
- 1 teaspoon dried basil
- 1 teaspoon dried thyme
- 1 teaspoon ground cumin
- ¼ teaspoon ground allspice
- 8 to 10 cups beef stock
- 2 tablespoons Worcestershire sauce
- 2 teaspoons sugar
- ½ cup chopped flat-leaf parsley
- 2 tablespoons seeded and finely diced hot chiles (1 medium jalapeño or 3 serranos)
- ¼ teaspoon finely diced fresh bird's eye chiles (do not seed; about 1 chile)
- ¾ cup chopped yellow onion
- 2 cups Baby Bliss or small Yukon Gold potatoes, quartered
- 1½ cups peeled parsnips or yams, cut into bite-size pieces
- 1 cup peeled carrots, cut into bite-size rounds
- 1 cup thinly sliced leeks (white and light green parts)
- 1 cup peeled turnip, cut into bite-size pieces
- 1½ cups celery, cut into bite-size pieces
- ¾ cup quartered button or small cremini mushrooms
- ¾ cup seeded and chopped red, green, or orange bell pepper

HERBED DUMPLINGS (OPTIONAL)

- 2 cups Bisquick baking mix
- ⅔ cup whole milk
- 2 tablespoons minced fresh flat-leaf parsley
- 1 tablespoon poppy or caraway seeds

1. Prepare the Beef Stew: Melt the shortening in a Lodge 7-quart cast iron Dutch oven over medium-high heat. Brown the meat well on all sides in batches. (Don't crowd the meat in the pan or it will steam and not brown.) Remove the meat to a plate as it is browned. When all the meat has been browned, return it to the pot, and season with the paprika and salt and pepper to taste. Add the garlic and tomato paste, and cook briefly, stirring to coat the meat with the paste. Add the roux, and cook, stirring, for 3 minutes. Add the bay leaves, rosemary, basil, thyme, cumin, allspice, and 4 cups of the stock. Stir to combine. Add the Worcestershire, sugar, and ¼ cup of the parsley. Add another 2 cups of the stock, and bring to a boil. Cover, reduce the heat to a simmer, and cook, stirring occasionally, until the meat is barely tender, about 45 minutes. Add the chiles, onion, potatoes, parsnips, carrots, leeks, and turnip. Add more stock and roux, if necessary, to cover the vegetables (add 1 tablespoon of the roux for every 2 cups stock). Cover and simmer for 20 minutes.

2. Add the celery, and cook for another 10 minutes. Add the mushrooms and bell pepper, and cook until the vegetables are tender, about another 5 minutes.

3. If serving with the dumplings, spoon out enough liquid into a small saucepan so the vegetables and meat are exposed. Keep the reserved liquid simmering over low heat while you make the dumpling dough. Keep the stew at a low boil.

4. If desired, prepare the Herbed Dumplings: In a medium bowl, combine all the dumpling ingredients until well mixed. Using two tablespoons, form the dough into oval-shaped, heaping tablespoon-sized dumplings, and drop onto the stew. (The dough will come off the spoons easier if the spoons are dipped in hot stock or water before forming.) Once all the dumplings have been added to the pot, cover and cook until a toothpick inserted into the dumplings comes out cleanly, 15 to 18 minutes. Transfer the dumplings to a warm plate, and keep warm in a low oven until ready to serve.

5. Return the reserved liquid to the pot, and stir to combine. Ladle the stew into warm serving bowls, and set several dumplings on top. Sprinkle with the remaining ¼ cup parsley, if desired.

A COOKING SECRET FROM MIKE

You can make your own dark roux (cook flour and unsalted butter or vegetable shortening together in a one-to-one ratio over medium-low heat, stirring constantly, until it is the color of chocolate, which can take an hour or more), or buy it ready-made—try Savoie's Old Fashioned Roux, which you can purchase online.

The word *wash-tunk-ala* is from the Lakota Sioux and means dried deer or buffalo meat. This game-and-corn stew is one favored by the Plains Indians. There are many versions, this one from Holly Arnold Kinney, second-generation owner of The Fort restaurant just outside of Denver, Colorado. "As a little girl, my father, Sam Arnold, food historian and founder of The Fort, would make this over the campfire in the restaurant's courtyard," remembers Holly.

WASH-TUNK-ALA INDIAN STEW

Serves 6

2 tablespoons olive oil

6 wild onions, green onions, or scallions, cut diagonally into ¾-inch pieces

2 pounds jerked meat (buffalo, beef, deer, elk, or a combination), cut into bite-size pieces

4 large red potatoes, peeled and cut into bite-size pieces

2 medium carrots, cut into bite-size pieces

1 large red bell pepper, seeded and cut into bite-size pieces

3 ears reconstituted dried corn (see Kitchen Note) or 1 ear corn, shucked and cut into 1-inch-thick discs

Salt to taste

3 tablespoons New Mexican red chile powder

2 quarts beef broth

3 tablespoons cornmeal

1. Heat the oil in a Lodge 7-quart cast iron Dutch oven over high heat. Add the onions, and sauté until slightly browned and translucent. Add the meat, and slowly stir until it is seared brown. Add the potatoes, carrots, bell pepper, and corn. Add the salt to taste and the New Mexican red chile powder. Stir.

2. Add the broth. Add a little cold water to the cornmeal, mix to create a paste, and stir into the soup. Slowly simmer for 2 hours.

KITCHEN NOTE:

To reconstitute dried ears of corn, soak them in water to cover overnight, or until tender.

A COOKING SECRET FROM HOLLY

You can use fresh meat in the place of dried meat. If you use jerky, be sure to buy pure dried meat and not commercial jerky, which is full of additives. With jerky, you'll end up with a more chewy texture.

Jim Maturo once won first place in the People's Choice category in the Florida state chili cook-off with this recipe. If you like beans in your chili, use pinto beans and cook them separately.

JIM MATURO'S CHILI

Serves 4 to 6

- 1 tablespoon vegetable shortening
- 2 pounds beef chuck fillet steak, sirloin tip roast, or chuck, trimmed and cut into ½-inch cubes (or 2 pounds hamburger meat)
- 2 cups beef broth, plus more (optional)
- 2 cups chicken broth
- 1 (15-ounce) can tomato sauce or diced tomatoes
- 2 medium onions, diced
- 3 tablespoons pure ground red chiles (or substitute chili powder)
- 1 teaspoon cayenne pepper
- 1 tablespoon salt (2 teaspoons if you substitute chili powder for the ground red chiles)
- 3 tablespoons chili powder
- 1½ teaspoons ground cumin (1 tablespoon if you substitute chili powder for the ground red chiles)
- 2½ teaspoons minced garlic
- 1 teaspoon freshly ground black pepper
- Toppings: grated Cheddar or Parmesan cheese, chopped onions, and sliced jalapeño chiles (optional)

1. Heat the shortening in a Lodge 4-quart cast iron Dutch oven over medium heat. Add the beef and brown on all sides.

2. Add the broths, tomato sauce, onions, ground red chiles, cayenne, and salt. Bring to a boil, then cover and continue to boil until the meat is almost tender, about 45 minutes.

3. Stir in the chili powder, cumin, garlic, and black pepper. Reduce the heat to low, and cook 30 minutes. Adjust the consistency with more beef broth, if desired.

4. Top with the cheese, chopped onions, and jalapeños.

MAYA DAILEY'S CHILE VERDE
GREEN CHILE STEW

Serves 4 to 6

Maya Dailey is the founder and owner of Maya's Farm, located in the urban setting of Phoenix, Arizona. Maya supplies certified organic vegetables, herbs, flowers, and eggs to local markets, restaurants, and schools.

Chile verde is one of Maya's favorite comfort foods, which, not surprisingly, she makes with her own tomatillos and peppers, topping each bowl with a generous shower of torn fresh cilantro leaves.

¼ cup good-quality cold-pressed extra-virgin olive oil
½ cup all-purpose flour
Salt and freshly ground black pepper
2 pounds boneless pork shoulder, trimmed of excess fat (leave some on for good flavor) and cut into ½-inch cubes
2 tablespoons ground cumin
1 tablespoon ground Chimayo green chile powder (see Kitchen Note)
1 dried pasilla chile, seeded and chopped (see Kitchen Note)
½ cup chopped green onions

12 tomatillos, husked, rinsed, and finely chopped
2 medium yellow onions, finely chopped
2 serrano chiles, seeded and finely chopped
2 Anaheim chiles, seeded and finely chopped
1 green bell pepper, seeded and finely chopped
2 cups chicken stock (store-bought is fine)
1 (15-ounce) can or 2 cups green chiles (Maya uses Bueno brand, which is sold frozen and comes mild, hot, or extra hot)
1 bunch fresh cilantro

1. Heat the oil in a Lodge 5-quart cast iron Dutch oven over medium heat until sizzling.

2. While the oil heats, season the flour generously with the salt and pepper. Toss the pork cubes with the seasoned flour until well coated; shake off any excess. Add the floured cubes to the hot oil in batches, and cook until nicely browned on all sides, 5 to 10 minutes. Remove the pork to a plate as it browns.

3. Add the cumin, chile powder, and pasilla chile to the oil left in the pot, and stir to combine well; cook over low heat, stirring constantly, until you can smell their fragrance, about 1 minute. Add the green onions, tomatillos, yellow onions, fresh chiles, and bell pepper, and cook over medium heat, stirring a few times, until the onions are caramelized, about 30 minutes. Add the meat back to the pot, along with the stock and green chiles, and let simmer until the flavors come together and the pork is tender, about 45 minutes, although Maya says, "It can simmer forever—the longer you simmer, the better it gets!" Adjust the heat as needed to prevent any scorching on the bottom.

4. To serve, ladle into bowls, and tear the cilantro leaves right over the stew.

KITCHEN NOTE:
Shop for ground Chimayo chile and dried pasilla chiles online.

This recipe is from Louise "Lou" S. Fuller, wife of Ed Fuller, former president of the National Cornbread Festival, which is held each year in Lodge's hometown, South Pittsburg, Tennessee. Of course, Lou likes to serve this soup with hot cornbread!

SOUTHERN GREENS SOUP

Serves 4

- 2 tablespoons canola oil
- 1 medium onion, chopped
- 4 cups water
- 1 envelope dry vegetable soup mix (such as Knorr's)
- 2 pounds fresh turnip greens, washed, drained, and chopped
- 1 (20-ounce) can white beans, drained
- 1 (14- to 16-ounce) package Polish sausage, sliced
- Hot water (optional)

1. Heat the oil in a Lodge 7-quart cast iron Dutch oven over medium-high heat; add the onion, and cook until softened, stirring occasionally. Add the water and soup mix, stirring to combine. Bring to a boil, and simmer 5 minutes.

2. Add the turnip greens, and simmer 10 minutes.

3. Add the beans and sausage; simmer until the greens are tender, about 15 minutes. If you want the soup more "soupy," add hot water a little at a time until the desired consistency.

CHICKEN AND MUSHROOM STEW WITH WILD RICE

Serves 6

"This soothing, rustic dish gets its deep flavors from the old-school chicken and wild rice casserole and its technique from a country-style French braise," says Hunter Lewis, editor in chief at *Cooking Light* and *Food & Wine* magazines, who makes his in a battered Lodge 6-quart enameled cast iron Dutch oven. Hunter recommends using real wild rice rather than quick-cooking. "You want that nutty flavor and slightly chewy texture from the grain to help sop up all of the good chicken and gravy."

3 tablespoons extra-virgin olive oil
1 (2-ounce) slice country ham or 2 slices bacon, finely chopped
6 skinless, boneless chicken thighs, cut into 2-inch pieces
Kosher salt and freshly ground black pepper
4 cups button mushrooms, quartered
¼ cup white wine vinegar
1 carrot, finely chopped
1 medium onion, finely chopped

3 garlic cloves, finely chopped
1 bay leaf
3 tablespoons salted butter
¼ cup all-purpose flour
1 cup whole or skim milk
2½ cups chicken broth
½ teaspoon freshly grated nutmeg
½ teaspoon dry mustard
1 (4-ounce) box wild rice, cooked according to package directions
2 tablespoons chopped fresh flat-leaf parsley

1. Preheat the oven to 325°F.

2. Heat 1 tablespoon of the oil in a Lodge 5-quart cast iron Dutch oven over medium-high heat. Add the ham, and cook, stirring occasionally, until browned, about 6 minutes. Transfer the browned ham to a plate with a slotted spoon.

3. Add 1 tablespoon of the oil to the pot. Season the chicken with the salt and pepper. Working in 2 batches, sear the chicken until browned on both sides, about 6 minutes for each batch. Transfer the chicken to the plate with the ham.

4. Add the remaining 1 tablespoon oil and the mushrooms to the pot, and cook, stirring occasionally, until just softened, about 4 minutes. Transfer to the plate with the chicken and ham. Add the vinegar to deglaze, and cook until reduced by half, loosening any browned bits from the bottom of the pot with a wooden spoon. Stir in the carrot, onion, garlic, and bay leaf, and cook, stirring occasionally, until the onion is softened, about 6 minutes. Remove from the heat, and return the ham, chicken, mushrooms, and any juices accumulated on the plate to the pot.

5. Melt the butter in a medium saucepan over medium-low heat until bubbling. Add the flour, and cook, whisking constantly, 1 minute. Whisk in the milk, and cook, whisking often, until the sauce thickens and coats the back of a spoon, about 4 minutes. Whisk in the broth, nutmeg, and mustard, and cook until the sauce thickens again. Season with the salt and pepper to taste.

6. Pour the gravy over the chicken mixture. Stir to combine. Cover the Dutch oven, and bake until the chicken is very tender, about 45 minutes. Serve the stew ladled over the rice and sprinkled with the parsley. Remove the bay leaf before serving.

Maybe twice a year, cookbook author James Villas loves nothing more than to throw a special Brunswick stew party for eight or ten fellow stewheads. "I don't think I've ever used the exact same recipe twice—which is one reason cooking Brunswick stew is so much fun," James says. Typically, Jim makes the stew a day in advance. For optimum flavor, he uses a hefty stewing hen, but if that's not available, he suggests using two ordinary 3-pound chickens. He serves the stew with country ham biscuits, coleslaw, homemade pickled peaches, and, for dessert, a hot berry cobbler with scoops of vanilla ice cream on top. "Rarely is there a cup of stew left in the pot or a morsel of food left on the table!"

SOUTHERN BRUNSWICK STEW

Serves 8 to 10

- 4 bacon slices
- ¼ cup vegetable oil
- 1 (6-pound) chicken, cut into 8 pieces
- 2 medium onions, chopped
- 2 celery ribs (with leaves), chopped
- 1 carrot, chopped
- 1 medium smoked ham hock, trimmed
- 3 large ripe tomatoes, chopped and juices reserved
- 1 small dried red chile, seeded and minced
- 1 tablespoon Worcestershire sauce
- 1 teaspoon paprika
- Salt and freshly ground black pepper
- 1½ cups fresh or frozen corn kernels
- 1½ cups fresh or frozen sliced okra
- 1½ cups fresh or frozen baby lima beans
- 1½ cups mashed cooked potatoes (optional)

1. Place a large Lodge cast iron Dutch oven over medium-high heat. Add the bacon, and cook until crisp. Remove to paper towels to drain, reserving the drippings in the skillet; crumble the bacon, and set aside.

2. Add the oil to the bacon drippings in the pan, and heat over medium-high heat. Add the chicken, brown on all sides, and transfer to a platter. Reduce the heat to medium, and add the onions, celery, and carrot; cook 5 to 8 minutes, stirring occasionally.

3. Return the chicken to the pan, and add the ham hock, tomatoes with juices, chile, Worcestershire, paprika, and salt and pepper to taste. Add enough water to cover the ingredients by 1 inch, and stir.

Bring to a steady simmer, skimming any residue off the surface; cover and cook slowly until the chicken is very tender, 2½ to 3 hours. Skim any excess fat from the top.

4. Using a slotted spoon, transfer the chicken and ham hock to the platter; when cool enough to handle, remove and discard the bones and any skin. Shred the meats and return to the pan. Add the corn, okra, lima beans, and reserved bacon. Simmer, uncovered, about 1 hour, stirring every 10 minutes for the first half-hour and then frequently, to prevent the ingredients from scorching on the bottom of the pan.

5. Add the mashed potatoes, if desired, and cook, stirring, until the stew is thickened, about 15 minutes. Taste and, if necessary, adjust the seasoning. Ladle the stew into large soup bowls.

"Double the recipe, invite friends to bring the beer and lawn chairs, make a couple of skillets full of cornbread, and have a good time!" says local South Pittsburg resident and friend of Lodge Mike Gonce. If you do double the recipe, be sure to use a Lodge 7-quart cast iron Dutch oven.

TENNESSEE WHITE CHILI

Serves 6

- 1 tablespoon canola oil
- 1 cup chopped onion
- 1 teaspoon minced garlic
- 1½ pounds chopped cooked chicken breasts, cut into small cubes
- 3 (15-ounce) cans Great Northern beans, drained
- 2 tablespoons chopped fresh cilantro or 2 teaspoons dried cilantro
- 2 teaspoons ground cumin
- ¼ teaspoon salt
- ¼ teaspoon cayenne pepper
- Chicken broth (optional)
- Shredded Monterey Jack cheese and crushed tortilla chips (optional)

1. Heat the oil in a Lodge 5-quart cast iron Dutch oven over medium heat. Add the onion and garlic, and cook, stirring occasionally, until tender.

2. Stir in the chicken, beans, cilantro, cumin, salt, and cayenne, and simmer 30 minutes. If desired, you can add chicken broth to reach the desired consistency.

3. Ladle the chili into bowls, and sprinkle each serving with the cheese and crushed tortilla chips, if desired.

Cioppino is a classic San Francisco seafood stew thought to have originated when fishermen would "chip in" whatever they had to a common pot. This recipe for cioppino from Al Hernandez, the food and wine editor of *The Vine Times*, brings the flavorful treat home to you. The recipe includes recommended seafood, but feel free to experiment and "chip in" whatever seafood you have available or prefer.

CIOPPINO
SAN FRANCISCO ITALIAN FISH STEW

Serves 6 to 8

¼ cup olive oil

1 large yellow onion, chopped

½ teaspoon salt, plus more to taste

6 garlic cloves, finely chopped

1 teaspoon dried oregano

1 teaspoon dried basil

1 teaspoon red pepper flakes

¼ cup tomato paste

1 cup dry white wine

1 cup chicken stock

1 cup seafood stock or clam juice

1 (28-ounce) can peeled whole tomatoes, undrained

1 pound shrimp (16 to 20 count preferred)

1 pound scallops, preferably bay

1 pound mussels

1 pound clams

1 whole cleaned cooked Dungeness crab (about 2 pounds) or 2 pounds king crab legs, thawed if necessary

1 pound firm white fish fillets (such as cod, catfish, or halibut)

Freshly ground black pepper

1 loaf sourdough bread, sliced and toasted

1. Heat the oil in a large Lodge cast iron Dutch oven over medium heat. Add the onion and salt, and cook, stirring occasionally, until softened, about 10 minutes. Add the garlic, oregano, basil, and red pepper. Stir in the tomato paste, wine, and chicken and seafood stock. Crush the tomatoes; pick out any tomato skins, and add the tomatoes and juice to the pan. Reduce the heat to low, and simmer 30 minutes.

2. While the tomato mixture simmers, peel and devein the shrimp. Remove the tough crescent-shaped muscle from each scallop, if it's still attached. Scrub the mussels and clams, and debeard the mussels, if necessary. Discard any mussels or clams that won't close.

3. Add the shrimp, scallops, crab, and fish to the pan. Cover and cook 10 minutes. Add the mussels and clams; cover and cook until they open, another 5 to 8 minutes (discard any that won't open). Season with the salt and pepper to taste.

4. Serve the cioppino in bowls topped with a slice of the toasted sourdough bread.

NORTH CAROLINA DOWN EAST CLAM CHOWDER

Serves 10 to 12

- ¼ pound salt pork or slab bacon, sliced ¼ inch thick
- ½ cup chopped onion
- 4 cups water, or half water and half clam juice
- 1 teaspoon salt
- ¼ teaspoon freshly ground black pepper
- 1 quart coarsely chopped chowder clams
- 4 cups diced (½-inch) potatoes
- 2 dozen small clams in the shell, scrubbed (farm-raised from North Carolina are perfect)
- Milk, half-and-half, or light or heavy cream (optional)
- Sliced white bread (optional)
- Chopped fresh flat-leaf parsley for garnish
- Oyster crackers

1. Cook the salt pork in a Lodge 5-quart cast iron Dutch oven over medium heat until crisp. Remove the pork, and discard, reserving the rendered fat in the pot. Add the onion, and cook until tender (but don't let it color), about 5 minutes, stirring a few times. Pour in the water, then add the salt and pepper. Bring to a boil. Add the chowder clams, reduce the heat to low, and slowly simmer, uncovered, until the clams are tender, about 1 hour.

2. Add the potatoes, increase the heat to medium, and simmer until they are tender, about 20 minutes. During the last 10 minutes, add the clams in the shell, and cover the pot. Discard any open clams. Add the milk, if desired, to reach the desired consistency, right before serving, but give it enough time to warm (a couple of minutes usually works).

3. If you like, set a slice of bread in the bottom of each large shallow serving bowl, then ladle in the chowder, making sure to get a couple of the shell clams. Sprinkle evenly with the parsley, and serve with the oyster crackers.

No, it's not Down East Maine, but rather North Carolina. All along its Outer Banks and Southern Outer Banks you'll find this style of chowder. Somewhat akin to the chowders of Rhode Island, this style is more about the clams than the thick, cream-based chowders of New England. "It's a type of chowder that you'll find at a local's home," says Fred Thompson, a cookbook author, resident of Raleigh, North Carolina, and executive editor of *Edible Piedmont.*

How Fred Makes Chowder

1. The key to a good chowder is timing. Wait until the potatoes are fork-tender before adding the clams in the shell, because they don't take long to cook.

2. Be careful not to overcook the clams. They will be completely cooked when their shells open wide (about 10 minutes). Discard shells that remain closed.

3. To thicken this chowder like the locals do, place a slice of white bread in the bottom of each bowl before ladling the chowder into the bowl.

POULTRY

Poultry is a tried-and-true staple of the American diet—and for good reason. Any way you prepare the bird, whether grilled, fried, whole-roasted, or baked into a potpie—all of which are ways we prepare it here using cast iron—it pairs well with so many flavors and never fails to please.

LODGE-KELLERMANN FAMILY MEMORIES

Edith Lodge Kellermann's niece, Elizabeth Lodge Sherwood, remembers watching her aunt make these croquettes during the 1930s. Edith's oldest granddaughter, Carolyn Kellermann Millhiser, remembers the same croquette recipe being prepared by her grandmother for luncheons 15 or 20 years later. Edith's table would be set with flowers from her garden, round hand-crocheted place mats, white linen napkins in silver napkin rings, individual salt cellars, and blue willow china. "Gramma" taught her grandchildren how to set a table with the silverware placed the width of a thumb from the edge of the table. The tea wagon was to the right of the hostess at the head of the table. Once the dishes were served, they, along with pitchers of iced tea and ice water, were left on the tea wagon within easy reach if anyone wanted a second helping.

Company founder Joseph Lodge's daughter, Edith Lodge Kellermann, started her tradition of making these croquettes as a luncheon specialty during the Depression years.

CHICKEN CROQUETTES

Serves 6 to 8

- 2 or 3 tablespoons salted butter
- ¼ cup all-purpose flour
- Salt and black pepper
- 1 cup whole milk
- 2 cups cooked chicken, cut into very small pieces
- 1 tablespoon Worcestershire sauce
- ½ cup chopped fresh parsley
- 1 large egg, beaten
- ½ cup fine buttered breadcrumbs
- Vegetable oil

1. Melt the butter in a Lodge 8-inch cast iron skillet over medium heat. Add the flour and salt and pepper to taste, and stir for a few minutes, but don't let the roux color at all. Slowly pour in the milk, stirring constantly, until the white sauce thickens, about 5 minutes. Stir in the chicken, Worcestershire, and parsley.

2. Transfer the mixture to a medium bowl, and refrigerate. Place the beaten egg in a small bowl and the breadcrumbs on a plate. When the chicken mixture is cool, take a rounded tablespoon of the mixture for each croquette; first dredge it in the crumbs, then coat with the beaten egg, then dredge again in the crumbs. Refrigerate the croquettes in a single layer in a covered dish for several hours to firm up.

3. In a Lodge 10-inch cast iron skillet, heat 1 inch of the oil over medium to high heat. When the oil is hot, fry the croquettes in batches (you don't want to crowd them in the pan), turning them often, until they are golden brown. Drain on paper towels.

NEW ENGLAND CHICKEN POTPIE WITH BISCUIT CRUST

Serves 6

FILLING

- 2 tablespoons butter
- 2 medium onions, diced
- 1 celery rib, diced
- 1 large carrot, diced
- 3 cups cubed (1-inch) cooked chicken
- 1½ cups fresh or frozen green peas
- 1 cup diced fresh mushrooms
- Salt and freshly ground black pepper
- ¼ cup vegetable shortening
- ¼ cup all-purpose flour
- 1½ cups chicken broth
- 1 cup half-and-half

BISCUIT CRUST

- 2 cups all-purpose flour
- 1 tablespoon baking powder
- ½ teaspoon salt
- ¼ cup chilled vegetable shortening
- 1 cup whole milk

1. Grease a Lodge 2-quart cast iron serving pot.

2. Prepare the Filling: Melt the butter in the pot over medium heat; add the onions, celery, and carrot, and stir until the vegetables soften, about 5 minutes. Stir in the chicken, peas, and mushrooms; season to taste with the salt and pepper, and set aside.

3. In a heavy medium saucepan, melt the shortening over medium heat, sprinkle the flour over the top, and stir constantly for 3 minutes; don't let the roux color. Remove from the heat, and gradually add the broth and half-and-half, stirring constantly until well blended. Return the mixture to the heat, and cook, stirring constantly, until the sauce thickens. Pour over the chicken and vegetables in the prepared pot.

4. Preheat the oven to 425°F.

5. Prepare the Biscuit Crust: In a medium bowl, whisk the flour, baking powder, and salt together. Add the shortening, and cut it in with a pastry cutter or rub it into the flour with your fingertips until the mixture is mealy. Add the milk, and stir just until the dough forms a ball. Transfer to a lightly floured work surface, knead about 8 times, and pat the dough out about ⅓ inch thick. Cut the dough to fit the top of the prepared pot, drape it over the filling, and secure the edges by crimping them. Cut a few vents in the top with a sharp knife, and bake until the crust is nicely browned and the juices are bubbling up through the vents, about 25 minutes.

All-American chicken potpie most likely came to us via an early New England stew made with a sturdy biscuit crust and baked in a heavy cast iron pot or casserole. The original pie probably contained neither peas nor mushrooms, but few would argue that this later innovation isn't at least partly responsible for the dish's popular and long-lasting appeal all over the country. This version is from cookbook author James Villas.

ET'S HEALTHY GLUTEN-FREE FRIED CHICKEN STRIPS

Serves 6

According to private chef June Pagan, Elizabeth Taylor had a great sense of humor and was very generous with the people who worked for her. "When I first introduced my healthier version of fried chicken to ET," remembers June, "I explained that I would serve it in boneless finger-shaped strips. She asked me—quite quizzically—'How many fingers are you planning to serve me?' I advised her that 4 to 5 'fingers' would be a 4-ounce portion (the recommended serving under the Pritikin guidelines that I was utilizing to optimize her weight-loss initiative). She laughed as she replied, 'OK, as long as you don't serve me just one.'"

1 pound skinless, boneless chicken breasts

BUTTERMILK MARINADE
1 cup buttermilk
1 large garlic clove, minced
1 teaspoon garlic powder
½ teaspoon Cajun-style seasoned salt
⅛ teaspoon freshly ground black pepper
½ teaspoon Mrs. Dash or Spike Salt Free Seasoning (optional)

RICE FLOUR DREDGE
¾ cup brown rice flour
¼ cup cornstarch
1 tablespoon sweet paprika
½ teaspoon dried thyme
¼ teaspoon black pepper
½ teaspoon garlic powder
½ teaspoon onion powder
½ teaspoon Cajun-style seasoned salt
About ¼ cup grapeseed oil, for frying

1. Wash and pat dry the chicken breasts with paper towels. Place the breasts between two sheets of parchment or wax paper, and pound with a meat mallet or rolling pin to ¼- to ⅓-inch thickness. Cut across the chicken into finger-like strips; set aside.

2. Prepare the Buttermilk Marinade: In a medium bowl, combine all of the ingredients, and blend well. Add the chicken strips; blend to coat them well. Cover and refrigerate for at least 1 hour or overnight.

3. Prepare the Rice Flour Dredge: When ready to fry, combine all of the ingredients (except the oil) in a medium bowl.

4. Heat a Lodge 10- or 12-inch cast iron skillet for 1 to 2 minutes over medium heat. Add just enough of the oil to coat the bottom by about ¼ inch. When the oil is hot (test by tossing a pinch of flour into the hot oil to see if it creates bubbles), commence with the next step.

5. Place one piece of chicken in the dredge, and coat it lightly and evenly; shake off any excess, and place it in the hot oil. You should see a line of bubbles form along the edges of the chicken. If you do, the oil is the proper temperature and you are ready to fry the rest of the chicken strips.

6. Quickly dredge the remaining chicken strips in the flour mixture in the same way. Add them to the hot oil, leaving about ½ inch of space between each strip; do not crowd the pan (you may need to fry them in batches). Fry until the bottoms are lightly browned and crisp to the touch, 4 to 5 minutes. Turn the strips over, and fry until the other side is golden brown, another 4 to 5 minutes.

7. Transfer the chicken to a paper towel-lined plate to drain. Test the strips to be sure the center is cooked through; it should be white, not pink. If the meat is still pink, finish cooking in a 400°F oven for 10 minutes.

This is one of Whendi Rose Grad's favorite ways to enjoy the honey she and her husband, Garnett Puett (a fourth-generation beekeeper), produce at Big Island Bees on the island of Kealakekua in Hawaii. Big Island Bees offers three single-floral varietals, made from the raw honey harvested by bees feasting off 'ohi'a lehua, macademia nut, or Christmasberry blossoms. Whendi likes to prepare this dish using their Organic Wilelaiki Blossom Honey, from the Christmasberry, but it's delicious prepared with any good-quality honey.

HONEY-ROASTED CHICKEN BREASTS WITH PRESERVED LEMON AND GARLIC

Serves 6

- 2 large skin-on, bone-in chicken breasts (about 2½ pounds)
- 1½ teaspoons fine sea salt
- Freshly ground black pepper to taste
- ¾ teaspoon ground cumin
- 1 preserved lemon, cut into quarters, flesh cut away from the rind and discarded (use only the rind)
- ¼ cup good-quality honey
- 2 tablespoons extra virgin olive oil
- 1 tablespoon unsalted butter
- 10 garlic cloves, crushed and halved

1. Preheat the oven to 375°F.

2. Season the chicken with the salt and pepper, and sprinkle the cumin both under and on the skin. Carefully tuck 2 quarters of the preserved lemon rind under the skin of each breast. Pour the honey under and over the top of the skin of each.

3. Heat a Lodge 10-inch cast iron skillet over medium-high heat for a few minutes (you want to get the skin really crunchy and brown). Add the oil and butter to the skillet; when the oil is hot and the butter melted, add the chicken, skin side down. Arrange the garlic in the pan so the cloves all make contact with the bottom. Cook for 7 minutes, then turn the chicken, skin side up, and transfer the skillet to the oven. Bake until the chicken is cooked through and the juices run clear, about 25 minutes.

4. Remove the skillet from the oven, and let the chicken cool in the pan for 5 minutes. Serve the chicken cut off the bone with all of the caramelized garlic pieces and the thick honey sauce.

A resident of South Pittsburg, Tennessee, Lodge's hometown, Wayne Gray, with his horse, Lady, participates in Civil War reenactments as an East Tennessee Federalist.

GRILLED CHICKEN WITH CITRUS SALSA

Serves 4

- 1 jalapeño chile, sliced
- ¼ cup plus 1 tablespoon fresh lime juice
- ¼ cup plus 1 tablespoon olive oil
- 4 skinned and boned chicken breasts
- Salt and freshly ground black pepper
- 1 navel orange, sectioned and cut into ¼-inch pieces
- 1 small grapefruit, sectioned and cut into ¼-inch pieces
- 4 green onions, thinly sliced
- 10 cherry tomatoes, seeded and diced
- Grated zest of ½ orange
- Grated zest of ½ lime
- 1 jalapeño chile, minced
- 4 handfuls mixed greens

1. Combine the jalapeño slices with ¼ cup each of the lime juice and oil in a shallow bowl.

2. Rub the chicken with the salt and pepper to taste, and place in the jalapeño marinade, turning to coat both sides. Cover and refrigerate 30 minutes.

3. Combine the orange and grapefruit pieces, green onions, tomatoes, orange and lime zest, minced jalapeño, the remaining 1 tablespoon each lime juice and oil, and salt and pepper to taste. Set the salsa aside.

4. Remove the chicken from the marinade; discard the marinade. Grease a Lodge 10½-inch square cast iron grill pan, and heat over medium-high heat until hot. Add the chicken, and cook 5 minutes on each side, until done. Remove the cooked chicken from the pan, and let stand 5 minutes.

5. Divide the greens among 4 serving plates. Slice each chicken breast, and place over the greens on each plate. Spoon the salsa over the top, and serve immediately.

On busy weeknights, Nashville-based Matt Moore, author of *The South's Best Butts: Pitmaster Secrets for Southern Barbecue Perfection*, among other books, still finds time to put together a wholesome, healthy meal. The versatility of cast iron allows Matt to create a perfect sear on skin-on, bone-in chicken breasts on the stove-top—then he finishes the dish off with the remaining ingredients by roasting everything in the oven. This meld of flavors tastes like it took hours of preparation when, truth be told, the meal can be prepped, cooked, and served in about a half hour. (Also pictured on the front cover)

PAN-ROASTED CHICKEN BREASTS WITH TOMATOES AND WHITE BEANS

Serves 2

- 2 tablespoons extra-virgin olive oil
- 2 (8-ounce) skin-on, bone-in chicken breasts
- 1 cup cherry tomatoes
- 4 garlic cloves, peeled
- Kosher salt and freshly cracked pepper
- ½ tablespoon dried rosemary
- 1 cup canned Great Northern, navy, or other white beans, rinsed and drained

1. Preheat the oven to 425°F.
2. Heat a Lodge 12-inch cast iron skillet over medium-high heat for 1 minute. Add the oil; heat until it shimmers in the pan and just begins to smoke. Add the chicken breasts, skin side down, and sear for 3 minutes (leave them totally alone, no fussing or poking). After 3 minutes, flip the chicken breasts; add the tomatoes and garlic so they make contact with the pan. Season everything lightly with salt and pepper, and sprinkle with the rosemary.
3. Place the skillet in the oven, and bake until the chicken is just cooked through at its thickest point, 18 to 22 minutes. Add the beans for the last 5 minutes of cooking, stirring them together with the tomatoes and garlic.
4. Remove the skillet from the oven; serve, discarding the garlic cloves.

In 1963 Catherine Kellermann, the youngest child of Edith and Charles Richard Kellermann and granddaughter of company founder Joseph Lodge, returned to South Pittsburg, Tennessee, to live with her elderly mother in the Lodge home. In the ensuing years, Catherine opened her home to her 18 nieces and nephews and their children, especially during the gathering of the Lodge family for the annual shareholders meeting. Chicken Piquant was her signature dish for smaller family gatherings.

CHICKEN PIQUANT

Serves 4

- 1 pound fresh mushrooms, sliced
- 4 skin-on, bone-in chicken breasts or leg quarters
- 2 tablespoons cornstarch or all-purpose flour
- ¼ cup water
- ¾ cup rosé wine
- ¼ cup soy sauce
- 2 tablespoons olive oil
- 2 tablespoons light brown sugar
- 1 garlic clove, crushed
- ¼ teaspoon dried oregano
- Hot cooked white rice

1. Preheat the oven to 350°F.

2. Lightly grease a Lodge 12-inch cast iron skillet. Scatter the mushrooms evenly over the bottom. Set the chicken pieces on top.

3. In a small bowl, mix the cornstarch and water together. Mix in the wine, soy sauce, 2 tablespoons oil, brown sugar, garlic, and oregano, and pour over the chicken. Bake, uncovered, until the chicken is tender and cooked through, 1 to 1½ hours, basting with the pan juices occasionally. Serve with the rice.

Cookbook author and *Bon Appétit* magazine contributing editor Dede Wilson has made this with both boneless, skinless chicken thighs as well as chicken breasts. You can also substitute white wine for the red for a slightly less dark and rich dish. Serve it with rice or steamed potatoes—or, better yet, the next day with crusty bread.

CHICKEN WITH ARTICHOKE HEARTS, OLIVES, AND CAPERS

Serves 4

8 skinned and boned chicken thighs or 2 skinned and boned chicken breasts (cut breasts into halves, and then cut in half crosswise)

Salt and freshly ground black pepper

2 tablespoons olive oil

1 large yellow or white onion, chopped

6 garlic cloves, minced

1 teaspoon fresh thyme leaves, crushed

¾ cup dry red wine

1 (28-ounce) can diced tomatoes, undrained

2 tablespoons balsamic vinegar

1 (9-ounce) package frozen artichoke hearts, thawed

¼ cup pitted green olives, such as Greek or French in brine, cut in half

¼ cup pitted black olives, such as kalamata, cut in half

2 tablespoons drained capers

¼ cup chopped fresh flat-leaf parsley

1. Season the chicken with the salt and pepper to taste. Heat the oil in a Lodge 5-quart cast iron Dutch oven over medium-high heat. Brown the chicken, a few pieces at a time, 4 minutes total for each batch (2 minutes for breasts). Remove the browned chicken pieces to a platter.

2. Add the onion to the pot, and cook, stirring occasionally, over medium-low heat until translucent and beginning to lightly brown, about 4 minutes. Add the garlic and thyme, and cook 1 minute. Add the wine, and bring to a boil, scraping the bottom of the pan to loosen the browned bits and incorporate them into the liquid. Stir in the tomatoes and vinegar.

3. Return the chicken to the pan, and add the artichokes, both kinds of olives, and the capers. Cover and simmer over medium-low heat until the chicken is done, about 30 minutes. Sprinkle with the parsley, and serve.

Tools matter, even for simple recipes, says Elaine Corn, cookbook author and contributing food and lifestyle reporter for Capital Public Radio in Sacramento, California. For her chicken-fried chicken, a cast iron skillet is a must, as well as paper towels, wax paper or plastic wrap, a meat mallet or rolling pin, a sheet of aluminum foil, and a reliable thermometer to measure the temperature of the frying oil.

CHICKEN-FRIED CHICKEN WITH CREAM GRAVY AND MASHED POTATOES

Serves 4

CHICKEN

- 1 cup buttermilk
- 4 to 6 drops hot sauce
- 4 skinless, boneless chicken breast halves
- 1 cup all-purpose flour
- 1 teaspoon salt, or to taste
- 1 teaspoon freshly ground black pepper, or more to taste

Mashed Potatoes (recipe at right)
Vegetable oil, for frying

CREAM GRAVY

- ¼ cup all-purpose flour
- 1 cup whole milk

Salt
Generous amount freshly ground black pepper (it should be peppery)

1. Prepare the Chicken: In a medium bowl, combine the buttermilk and hot sauce.

2. Rinse the chicken breasts, and pat dry with paper towels. One at a time, sandwich a breast between two sheets of wax paper or plastic wrap. Pound until thin and of even thickness. If you don't have a meat mallet, pound the breasts with a rolling pin. Add the pounded breasts to the buttermilk, turning to coat them if necessary. Let stand 20 to 60 minutes at room temperature.

3. Meanwhile, line a dinner plate or baking sheet with wax paper. To a paper bag, add the flour, salt, and pepper. Shake to mix well. Place the breasts, one at a time, in the paper bag, and shake until coated with the seasoned flour. Place the breasts in a single layer on the lined dinner plate. Let the coating set about 20 minutes. Meanwhile, start the mashed potatoes. Warm a serving platter in a preheated 150°F oven. Line another plate with two thicknesses of paper towels, and have it convenient to the stove.

4. Heat a Lodge 12-inch cast iron skillet over medium-high heat. When hot, pour in the oil to a depth of 1 inch. Heat to 350°F to 375°F. Slip the breasts into the hot oil. Don't crowd, or they will stick. Adjust the heat to keep it at an even temperature. Fry the chicken until golden brown, crusty, and crisp on both sides, turning with tongs, about 5 minutes per side. Drain on the paper towels. Transfer the breasts to the warm platter, cover loosely with aluminum foil, and keep warm in the 150°F oven while you make the gravy.

5. Prepare the Cream Gravy: Pour off all but 3 tablespoons of oil from the skillet. Return the skillet to medium-high heat. Add the flour, and whisk well until the roux is completely smooth, about 1 minute; don't let it take on any color! Be sure to loosen and scrape up any crusty bits that may be stuck to the bottom of the pan. Slowly add the milk, whisking constantly until there are no lumps. Season with the salt and pepper to taste. Reduce the heat to low, and simmer, stirring, until slightly thickened, about 5 minutes.

6. To serve, arrange the chicken and a serving of mashed potatoes on 4 dinner plates. Ladle on the cream gravy until smothered.

MASHED POTATOES

Serves 4

- 4 russet potatoes, peeled and cut into chunks
- 2 tablespoons unsalted butter
- ½ cup milk or heavy cream
- Salt and freshly ground black pepper

1. Bring a pot of salted water to a boil, drop in the potato chunks, cover, reduce the heat to medium, and cook until a knife easily glides into a potato chunk, 12 to 15 minutes.

2. Pour off the water, and return the pot to low heat to dry out the potatoes a bit. Add the butter, milk, salt to taste, and lots of pepper. Whisk by hand or with a handheld electric mixer until smooth. Keep warm until ready to serve.

"In my family, favorite dishes are always being altered according to what is available and what is best—especially when I'm cooking," says Lidia Bastianich, restaurateur, best-selling cookbook author, and one of the best-loved chefs on television. "Here's a perfect example: Chicken and potatoes, fried together in a big skillet so they're crisp and moist at the same time, is my mother's specialty. Growing up, my brother and I demanded it every week; our kids, Tanya, Joe, Eric, Paul, and Estelle, clamored for it, too. And now the next generation of little ones is asking their great-grandmother to make chicken and potatoes for them."

MY MOTHER'S CHICKEN AND POTATOES (WITH MY SPECIAL TOUCHES)

Serves 4 to 6

BASIC CHICKEN AND POTATOES

- 2½ pounds skin-on, bone-in chicken legs or assorted pieces
- ½ cup canola oil
- ½ teaspoon kosher salt, or more to taste
- 1 pound Red Bliss potatoes, preferably no bigger than 2 inches across
- 2 tablespoons extra-virgin olive oil, or more as needed
- 2 medium-small onions, quartered lengthwise
- 2 short sprigs fresh rosemary with plenty of needles

LIDIA'S SPECIAL TOUCHES (TRY EITHER OR BOTH)

- 4 to 6 ounces sliced bacon (5 or 6 slices)
- 1 or 2 pickled cherry peppers, sweet or hot (or none, or more!), cut in half and seeded

1. Rinse the chicken pieces, and pat dry with paper towels. Trim off the excess skin and all visible fat. Cut the drumsticks from the thighs. If using breast halves, cut each into 2 smaller pieces.

2. If using the bacon, make roll-ups: Cut the bacon slices in half crosswise, and roll each half into a neat, tight cylinder. Stick a toothpick through the roll to secure it; cut or break the toothpick so only a tiny bit sticks out.

3. Pour the canola oil into a Lodge 15-inch cast iron skillet, and set over high heat. Sprinkle the chicken on all sides with ¼ teaspoon of the salt. When the oil is very hot, lay the pieces, skin side down, an inch or so apart—watch out for oil spatters. Don't crowd the chicken: If necessary, fry it in batches, similar pieces (like drumsticks) together. Drop the bacon rolls into the oil around the chicken, turning and shifting them often. Let the chicken fry in place for several minutes to brown on the underside, then turn and continue frying

until it's golden brown on all sides, 7 to 10 minutes or more for dark meat pieces. Fry the breast pieces only for 5 minutes or so, taking them out of the oil as soon as they are golden. Let the bacon rolls cook and get lightly crisp, but not dark. Adjust the heat to maintain steady sizzling and coloring; remove the crisped chicken pieces and bacon rolls with tongs to a bowl.

4. Meanwhile, rinse and dry the potatoes; slice each one through the middle on the axis that gives the largest cut surface, and toss them in a bowl with the olive oil and remaining ¼ teaspoon salt.

5. When the chicken and bacon are cooked and out of the skillet, pour off the frying oil. Return the skillet to medium heat, and put all the potatoes, cut side down, in a single layer in the hot pan. With a rubber spatula, scrape all the olive oil out of the bowl back into the skillet; drizzle over a bit more oil if the pan seems dry. Fry and crisp the potatoes for about 4 minutes to form a crust, then move them around the pan, still cut side down, until they're all brown and crisp, 7 minutes or more. Turn them over, and fry another 2 minutes to cook and crisp on their rounded skin sides.

6. Still over medium heat, toss the onion wedges and rosemary sprigs around the pan with the potatoes. If using the cherry peppers, cut the seeded halves into ½-inch-wide pieces, and scatter them in the pan, too. Return the chicken pieces—except the breast pieces—to the pan, along with the bacon rolls; pour in any chicken juices that have accumulated in the bowl. Raise the heat slightly, and carefully turn and tumble the chicken, potatoes, onions, bacon, and pepper pieces, so they're heating up and getting coated with pan juices—but take care not to break the potato pieces. Spread everything out in the pan—the potatoes on the bottom as much as possible so they can keep crisping up—and put on the cover.

7. Lower the heat to medium, and cook for about 7 minutes, shaking the pan occasionally; uncover and tumble everything again. Cover and cook another 7 minutes or so, then add the breast pieces and give everything another tumble. Cover and cook for 10 minutes more.

8. Remove the cover, turn the pieces again, and cook in the open skillet for about 10 minutes to evaporate the moisture and caramelize everything. Taste a bit of the potato (or chicken) for salt, and sprinkle on more as needed. Turn the pieces now and then. When everything is all glistening and golden and the potatoes and chicken are cooked through, remove the skillet from the stove and—as Lidia does at home—bring it right to the table. Serve portions of chicken and potatoes, or let people help themselves.

A COOKING SECRET FROM LIDIA

Sticking a toothpick through each bacon roll to secure it will allow the bacon to roll around in the pan and cook evenly.

According to Honolulu-based culinary product specialist Ann Hall Every, this is one of the most popular foods in Hawaii when ordering a "plate lunch," which is not just for lunchtime eating. Drive-ins are a classic place to experience a plate lunch, as well as many other casual restaurants. A plate lunch comes with two scoops of rice (medium-grain white rice scooped with an ice-cream scoop) and a scoop of macaroni salad, which in Hawaii sometimes includes cooked cubed potatoes.

SHOYU CHICKEN

Serves 4 to 6, depending on the size of the chicken thighs

- 1 cup shoyu (see Kitchen Note)
- 1 cup water
- ¼ cup mirin (sweet cooking wine)
- ⅓ cup firmly packed dark brown sugar
- ⅓ cup granulated sugar
- 6 garlic cloves, finely minced
- 1 tablespoon minced fresh ginger (no need to peel)
- 1 teaspoon freshly ground black pepper
- 1 teaspoon red pepper flakes
- 12 skin-on, bone-in chicken thighs (preferably organic)

1. In a glass or ceramic dish large enough to hold the chicken in a single layer, mix together the shoyu, water, mirin, both sugars, garlic, ginger, and black and red pepper; stir to dissolve the sugars.
2. Place the chicken thighs in the marinade, turning to coat them; cover with plastic wrap, and refrigerate for up to 12 hours. Remove from the refrigerator 1 hour before grilling.
3. Heat a Lodge 12-inch cast iron grill pan over medium-high heat for 5 minutes. Lightly pat dry the chicken, and place in the hot grill pan, skin side down. Lower the heat to medium-low, and grill until the chicken is cooked through, about 15 minutes per side.

KITCHEN NOTE:

Shoyu is the Japanese name for soy sauce. You can use a reduced-sodium version, if desired.

Come summer, it's too hot to cook inside. Instead of grilling up the usual suspects, try this beer can chicken from Max Brody, former chef/owner of The Night Kitchen in Montague, Massachusetts and owner of The Buxton Common in Buxton, Maine. The beer helps to keep the meat moist and flavorful, while the heat from the coals creates a crispy and delicious exterior. The cast iron pan gives your beer can–ensconced chicken added stability on the grill, plus the chicken benefits from the extra moisture provided by the beer evaporating from the pan.

CAST IRON BEER CAN CHICKEN

Serves 4, or 2 with leftovers

½ cup (1 stick) butter, melted
2 tablespoons soy sauce
1 tablespoon Dijon mustard
1 tablespoon light brown sugar
Salt and freshly ground black pepper

1 (3- to 4-pound) whole chicken, giblets removed
2 (12-ounce) cans beer of your choice

1. Start the coals in a chimney. Whisk together the melted butter, soy sauce, mustard, brown sugar, and salt and pepper to taste. Rub the marinade over the outside and inside of the chicken.

2. When the coals are hot, pour them on the bottom rack of your grill and arrange them around the perimeter of the grate, creating an area of indirect heat in the center.

3. Open 1 can of beer, and place it on a large Lodge cast iron skillet. Place the chicken on top of the can so that the can is inside the cavity of the bird, with the bird sitting upright on the can. Place the skillet on the grill, over the area of indirect heat. Open the remaining can of beer, and pour half of it into the skillet.

4. Partially close the grill lid. Check the chicken occasionally to make sure there is always liquid in the skillet, adding more of the remaining beer as needed. Baste the chicken with the juices that accumulate in the pan. Cook until a meat thermometer inserted into the thickest portion of the thigh registers 165°F, about 1 hour and 20 minutes. Remove the skillet with the chicken from the grill, and let cool for a few minutes before carefully removing the chicken from the beer can. (Be careful: The can will still be hot.)

5. Open a few more beers and enjoy!

HAY-ROASTED CHICKEN

Serves 4

- 3 ounces country white bread, cut into 1-inch cubes
- ⅓ cup buttermilk (Tyler likes to use Cruze Farm Dairy buttermilk from Knoxville, Tennessee)
- 3 garlic cloves, crushed
- 3 golden shallots, coarsely chopped
- 2½ tablespoons extra-virgin olive oil
- 5 tablespoons rendered duck fat or unsalted butter
- 3 tablespoons chopped fresh flat-leaf parsley
- 1 tablespoon coarsely chopped fresh rosemary
- 1 ounce sprigs fresh thyme
- 2 tablespoons whole-grain mustard
- Kosher salt and freshly ground black pepper
- 1 (2½-pound) roasting chicken
- 2 handfuls unsprayed wheat straw, moistened with water
- Finely grated zest of 2 lemons
- Finely grated zest of 2 oranges
- 10 star anise
- 2 tablespoons fennel seeds
- 2 tablespoons coriander seeds
- 1 tablespoon canola oil

This is a recipe from Tyler Brown, former executive chef of the Capitol Grille at The Hermitage Hotel in Nashville, Tennessee.

1. Preheat the oven to 350°F.

2. In a medium bowl, combine the bread and buttermilk; let stand until the bread softens, about 5 minutes. Drain, and then squeeze the excess buttermilk from the bread.

3. In a covered Lodge 10-inch cast iron skillet over low heat, sweat the garlic and shallots in 1½ tablespoons of the olive oil, stirring occasionally, until tender, about 10 minutes. Let cool, then transfer the mixture to a food processor or blender. Add the bread, duck fat, 1 tablespoon of the parsley, the rosemary, and thyme, and process into a paste. Stir in the remaining 1 tablespoon olive oil and 2 tablespoons parsley and the mustard, and season to taste with the salt and pepper.

4. Gently separate the skin from the chicken breasts with your fingers, being careful not to tear it. Spoon in a little of the stuffing, and spread it evenly across each breast by gently running your hand over the skin to smooth it out. Spoon the remaining stuffing into the cavity of the bird. Truss the cavity closed with kitchen twine. Season the chicken with the salt and pepper to taste, and set aside.

5. Combine the moist straw, citrus zest, star anise, and fennel and coriander seeds in a Lodge 7-quart cast iron Dutch oven.

6. Heat the canola oil in a Lodge 12-inch cast iron skillet over high heat, and brown the chicken well on all sides. Place the browned chicken on top of the hay mixture, cover, and bake until the juices run clear at the thigh when pierced, about 1½ hours. Let stand for 10 minutes before carving into serving pieces.

A COOKING SECRET FROM TYLER

Roasting the chicken in wheat straw allows it to retain its moisture and develop a very earthy flavor. Purchase unsprayed wheat straw from a local farmers' market or feed store.

SKILLET ROAST CHICKEN

Serves 4 to 6

John Schenck, publisher of *Edible Rhody* magazine, always roasts his chicken in a cast iron skillet. "I know roast chicken recipes are a dime a dozen, but this one provides guaranteed moist breast meat and great pan juices," he maintains. A key to the recipe's success is that the chicken just fits in the pan. The heat radiating from the raised rim of the skillet helps ensure that the legs cook as fast as the breast and that the skin browns uniformly. A 9- or 10-inch pan should work for a 4-pound chicken.

1 (3½- to 4-pound) roasting chicken
3 tablespoons cold butter
1 lemon
1 or 2 garlic cloves, peeled
2 or 3 sprigs fresh rosemary
Salt and freshly ground black pepper
2 tablespoons softened butter
½ teaspoon smoked Spanish paprika
Wine, chicken broth, or water (optional)

1. Preheat the oven to 450°F. Pull the liver, gizzard, and other innards from the cavity of the chicken, and save for another use or discard. Rinse and dry the chicken inside and out with paper towels. Remove the flaps of fat from the cavity opening—there should be one on each side. (If your butcher has removed the fat, you can use cold butter for this step. Figure on 1 tablespoon for each breast.) Cut each piece of fat in half. Work your fingers under the skin of each breast, being careful not to tear it, going as far back as you can. Put two pieces of the cavity fat under the skin on each breast, one in the back, toward the wing, the other farther forward near the leg. Position them fairly high up so that, as the chicken cooks, they melt down over and into the breast meat, keeping it moist.

2. Pierce the lemon with a poultry needle to make about 12 holes. Insert the lemon in the cavity. Next, place the garlic, rosemary, and a little salt and pepper inside, and close up the cavity with the needle.

3. Rub the chicken all over with about half of the softened butter, then sprinkle it with the paprika and salt and pepper.

How John Roasts a Chicken

1. Use kitchen shears to remove the flaps of fat from both sides of the cavity opening—there should be one on each side—and to cut each piece in half.

2. Gently use your fingers to push the pieces of fat under the skin without tearing it. If the skin tears, the fat will melt into the pan instead of directly into the meat.

3. Stuff the cavity with ingredients such as rosemary, garlic, and lemon. Use a poultry needle to close the cavity so that the flavors will be trapped in the cavity and infuse into the meat while baking.

4. Place the chicken in a heated skillet with melted butter. The skillet needs to be small enough so that the legs almost touch the sides of the skillet. Try a 9- or 10-inch Lodge cast iron skillet.

4. Heat the remaining half of the softened butter in a Lodge 9- or 10-inch cast iron skillet over high heat. Once the butter has melted and is sizzling, put the chicken in the pan, breast side up. It should fit snugly, with the legs almost touching the wall of the pan. If they do touch, that's fine. Let the chicken sizzle in the pan for a minute or two, then place it in the oven. Bake for 30 minutes, then turn off the oven, and let rest for another 30 minutes. Do not open the oven.

5. Take the pan out of the oven, and let the chicken rest in it for at least 20 minutes. With an instant-read thermometer, check the internal temperature at the thigh; it should be 165°F. Transfer the chicken to a serving platter. Carve it, and cover with aluminum foil to keep it warm while you heat up the pan juices—add a little wine, chicken broth, or water, if desired. Let it boil for a couple of minutes; turn off the heat, and stir in the remaining 1 tablespoon cold butter, whisking or stirring until it melts into the juices. Serve the chicken pieces with the pan juices poured over.

BUTTERMILK-BRINED FRIED CHICKEN WITH HOT PEPPER HONEY

Serves 6

Hot Pepper Honey (recipe at right)
Southern Buttermilk Brine (recipe at right)
1 (4-pound) whole chicken, cut into 8 pieces

SEASONED FLOUR
2½ cups all-purpose flour
1 tablespoon kosher salt
2 teaspoons coarsely ground black pepper
2 teaspoons granulated garlic
2 teaspoons onion powder
2 teaspoons smoked Spanish paprika
1 quart peanut oil

North Carolina native Elizabeth Karmel, is the executive chef of Hill Country Barbecue Market in New York City, Brooklyn, and Washington, D.C., and of Hill Country Chicken in New York City and Brooklyn. She serves her fried chicken with spicy honey. "The hot pepper honey is a variation on the theme of one of my Southern staples, hot pepper jelly. It elevates the chicken, adding a fiery sweetness that captures the best of Southern fried chicken in one bite!" says Elizabeth. You can also melt down hot pepper jelly for the same effect.

1. Prepare the Hot Pepper Honey (preferably several days in advance to let the flavors develop) and the Southern Buttermilk Brine.
2. Pat the chicken pieces dry, and remove the excess fat. Place the chicken in a heavy-duty brining bag or a nonreactive food-safe container with a lid. Pour the brine on the chicken, cover, and refrigerate for 2 to 3 hours. The smaller pieces will take less time and the larger pieces will take more time. DO NOT OVERBRINE or the chicken will be too salty.
3. Prepare the Seasoned Flour: In a medium bowl, whisk all of the ingredients together.
4. Remove the chicken from the brine; drain off the excess liquid. Coat evenly in the seasoned flour, shaking off any excess. Let stand for 5 minutes, then coat again with the seasoned flour, and let stand another 5 minutes before frying.
5. Pour enough oil in a Lodge 5-quart cast iron Dutch oven to reach ¼ inch up the side. Heat the oil to 325°F. You may have to adjust the heat level under the pot to maintain a steady temperature.
6. Immediately place the chicken, skin side down, in the hot oil, and cover the pot. Once you see that the bottoms of the chicken pieces are golden brown and the tops are beginning to cook, about 10 minutes, turn the chicken over. Place the lid back on the pot, and fry for another 5 minutes or so. You can remove the lid when the chicken is almost done to crisp up the skin. Cook a total of 20 to 25 minutes, depending on the size of the chicken pieces. Remember, turn only once; larger pieces may take longer. The chicken should be cooked all the way to the bone. Note: It may help to place the thighs in the middle of the pot where the oil is the hottest, and surround them with the breasts, legs, and wings.
7. Drain the chicken on a wire rack set on a baking sheet, and place in a low oven (250°F to 300°F) until ready to serve. Serve with the Hot Pepper Honey on the side.

HOT PEPPER HONEY

Makes about 1¼ cups

¼ cup favorite fruity hot sauce, preferably habañero

1 to 2 generous teaspoons red pepper flakes, to your taste

Pinch of fine sea salt

1 cup best-quality honey

In a small bowl, mix all the ingredients together well. Taste and adjust the level of heat to your liking. Store in a glass jar in the refrigerator. This gets better after it stands for a couple of days. It will keep for up to a week. Stir before using.

SOUTHERN BUTTERMILK BRINE

Makes about 2 quarts

3 cups hot water

1 cup kosher salt

1 cup firmly packed dark brown sugar

2 tablespoons dried rosemary or 3 large sprigs fresh rosemary

1 generous teaspoon cracked black peppercorns

2 generous cups ice cubes

4 cups cold buttermilk

1 teaspoon cayenne pepper

1. In a large saucepan over high heat, bring the water, salt, sugar, rosemary, and peppercorns to a boil, stirring to dissolve the sugar and salt. Stir and let steep and cool for 15 minutes.

2. Add the ice cubes, buttermilk, and cayenne. Whisk well.

How Elizabeth Fries Chicken

1. For an extra crispy crust, coat the chicken pieces twice in the seasoned flour. After each coat, let the chicken stand for 5 minutes.

2. Be sure the oil reaches 325°F before frying the chicken. To see if the oil has reached the right temperature, drop a cube of bread in the oil. If it floats and immediately starts to bubble and brown on the edges, then the oil is ready.

3. Carefully place the chicken in the hot oil. Keep the pot covered while frying and only remove it once the chicken is almost done. This final step will ensure the skin gets crisp.

4. Remove the chicken from the oil, and drain on a wire rack set on a baking sheet. Keep warm in an oven heated at 250°F to 300°F until ready to serve.

CAMP DUTCH OVEN COOKING

A camp Dutch oven is specifically designed for outdoor cooking. It has three stubby legs that lift it off the ground just enough so that hot coals can be set underneath it, as well as a flat, flanged lid so coals can be set on top of it with no worry that they will roll off. You can choose between shallow and deep camp Dutch ovens; they range in size from 8 to 16 inches in diameter. The shallow camp Dutch ovens are also known as "bread ovens," as they are the preferred pot when cooking bread or biscuits. The deeper camp Dutch ovens are perfect for chili, stews, and meat dishes.

CAMP COOKING 101

1. Prepare your cooking area. You want to choose a site with as much wind shelter as possible. If need be, build up a windbreak around where you will set your pot using patio stones, brick, or concrete block. If you are using a camp Dutch oven in your backyard, be sure to clear the cooking area of twigs and other flammable materials. You may also want to lay out an area of brick to use for your fire site.

2. Determine how many briquettes you'll need for the temperature you want, and get them going in a chimney starter. (See the chart below or your recipe.)

3. Place the hot coals. Draw an outline of the bottom of your pot where it will be cooking. Using the chart (or your recipe) as your guide, place the appropriate number of bottom briquettes in a checkerboard pattern within that outline. Set the oven over those coals. Then place the top coals in a checkerboard pattern on the lid of the oven, if your recipe calls for them.

4. Rotate your oven. To maintain an even oven temperature and prevent hot spots, lift and rotate the oven a quarter turn every 15 minutes. Then rotate the lid a quarter turn in the opposite direction. You'll find that a pair of welding gloves and a lid lifter are necessities for camp cooking.

BAKING IN YOUR CAMP DUTCH OVEN

OVEN SIZE	BRIQUETTES	325°F	350°F	375°F	400°F	425°F	450°F
8"	Total briquettes Top/bottom	15 10/5	16 11/5	17 11/6	18 12/6	19 13/6	20 14/6
10"	Total briquettes Top/bottom	19 13/6	21 14/7	23 16/7	25 17/8	27 18/9	29 19/10
12"	Total briquettes Top/bottom	23 16/7	25 17/8	27 18/9	29 19/10	31 21/10	33 22/11
14"	Total briquettes Top/bottom	30 20/10	32 21/11	34 22/12	36 24/12	38 25/13	40 26/14
16"	Total briquettes Top/bottom	37 25/12	39 26/13	41 27/14	43 28/15	45 29/16	47 30/17

Traditional Sunday chicken dinner is taken up a notch with this great dish. The orange glaze adds a perfect citrus touch to the hens and rice. Campfire cooking expert Johnny Nix says, "Serving these small hens keeps everyone from fighting over their favorite piece of the chicken."

ROAST CORNISH GAME HEN WITH WILD RICE STUFFING

Serves 6

2 tablespoons butter
1 medium onion, finely diced
1 cup finely diced celery
1 cup chopped mushrooms
1½ cups wild rice, cooked according to package directions using chicken broth instead of water
½ teaspoon dried thyme, crushed

½ teaspoon dried marjoram, crushed
Salt and freshly ground black pepper
1 (12-ounce) jar orange marmalade
½ cup orange juice
6 Rock Cornish game hens

1. Melt the butter in a large Lodge cast iron skillet over a medium fire. Add the onion, celery, and mushrooms, and cook, stirring occasionally, until tender. Remove from the fire, and let cool. Stir in the cooked rice, thyme, and marjoram, and season with the salt and pepper to taste.
2. In a small saucepan, bring the marmalade and orange juice to a boil, and cook until the mixture is reduced by half.
3. Stuff the cavity of each hen loosely with the rice mixture; tie the legs together, and place, breast side up, on a trivet in a Lodge 14-inch cast iron camp Dutch oven (an oven with a flat lid). Put the lid on, top with an even layer of coals, and roast over a campfire at medium heat (see Camp Dutch Oven Cooking, page 100; 350°F) until the juices run clear when cut at the joint between the leg and thigh, 45 minutes to 1 hour. Begin basting the hens with the marmalade glaze once they begin to brown; baste two or three times.

"Everything is better with bacon," says campfire cooking expert Johnny Nix. The wonderful flavor of bacon mixed with the herbs and cheese makes this dish a real crowd-pleaser.

BACON-WRAPPED STUFFED TURKEY BREAST

Serves 10

1 (3-pound) boneless turkey breast

¼ cup (½ stick) unsalted butter, softened

1 tablespoon mashed roasted garlic

2 teaspoons dried basil, crushed

1 (10-ounce) package frozen chopped spinach, thawed and squeezed dry

½ cup (2 ounces) shredded Asiago cheese

1 pound thin bacon slices

1. Place the turkey breast, skin side down, on a cutting board; spread the skin out as much as possible so it can wrap around the breast.
2. In a small bowl, stir together the butter, garlic, and basil. Spread the flavored butter over the inside of the breast. Arrange the spinach lengthwise down the center, and top with the cheese. Pull the skin around the breast, taking care not to tear it, to make a roll.
3. Lay the bacon slices on the cutting board, slightly overlapping each slice. Place the turkey breast on top of the bacon, and wrap the bacon around the breast. Make sure to overlap the ends of the strips; this will keep the bacon from curling as it cooks.
4. Place the turkey breast on a roasting rack inside a Lodge 14-inch cast iron camp Dutch oven (an oven with a flat lid). Put the lid on, top with an even layer of coals, and cook over a campfire at medium-high heat (see Camp Dutch Oven Cooking, page 100; 450°F) until a meat thermometer inserted in the center of the breast reads 170°F.
5. Remove the turkey breast from the oven, and let stand 10 minutes before carving.

At her former restaurant Scrimshaw in Greenport, New York, on the North Fork of Long Island, chef Rosa Ross offered duck breast served with a classic cherry sauce made with reduced duck stock—far too much work for the home cook. At home, Rosa will sauté ripe cherries or raspberries in a little duck fat, then sprinkle them with vinegar, the acidity bringing the perfect balance to the rich duck. "This is such a delicious and quick meal. Served with asparagus and parsleyed new potatoes, it makes a lovely spring dinner," says Rosa.

PAN-SEARED DUCK BREASTS WITH FRESH RASPBERRIES

Serves 4

- 2 whole (4 halves) skin-on, boneless duck breasts (about ½ pound each)
- Salt and freshly ground black pepper
- 1 pint fresh raspberries or pitted sweet or sour cherries, depending on what's in season
- 2 tablespoons raspberry vinegar
- ½ teaspoon sugar
- Fresh rosemary leaves

1. Preheat the oven to 350°F.

2. Score the duck skin in a diamond pattern, and sprinkle the breasts with the salt and pepper. Place the breasts, skin side down, in a Lodge 12-inch cast iron skillet. Set the skillet over medium heat, and cook until the skin is golden brown. Carefully pour off as much of the fat as possible, and refrigerate in a tightly covered container for a future use (like browning potatoes).

3. Turn the breasts over, skin side up, and place the skillet in the oven. Bake until the desired degree of doneness, 8 to 10 minutes for medium-rare. Transfer the duck breasts to a warm platter to stand at least 5 minutes. The breasts may then be sliced or left whole to serve.

4. Meanwhile, return the skillet to medium heat, add the raspberries, and cook just until they are beginning to burst, about 1 minute or less, depending on their ripeness. Sprinkle them with the vinegar and sugar, and toss to blend. Add a little water to deglaze the pan, scraping up the tasty browned bits from the bottom of the skillet. Pour over the duck breasts to serve. Sprinkle with the rosemary.

A CAST IRON MEMORY

In my everyday kitchen, my cast iron skillet is the first pan I reach for—for eggs, burgers, steaks, potatoes, and almost everything I want to sauté.

I "inherited" a set of skillets from a neighbor when we bought our house on the North Fork of Long Island. Until then, I had a 9-inch cast iron skillet that I had been working on for years to get just the right temper, but it was still a little "young." The pans I inherited were at least two generations old, and they were truly black and absolutely nonstick.

Years before, I had taken a class with James Beard, and he showed us how to cook hamburgers in a cast iron skillet: Heat the skillet to smoking, sprinkle a layer of salt in the bottom, and put in the patties, then cook the burgers till they release, and flip over. Cook to your desired degree of doneness, preferably rare to medium-rare. Needless to say, my patties have never stuck, and I've only gotten juicy, delicious results. An old black pan is essential to the perfect hamburger!

—Rosa Ross

Duck breast is a treat to enjoy at fine restaurants, but many people are hesitant to try it themselves at home. This recipe from Al Hernandez, food and wine editor of *The Vine Times*, helps you bring that tasty and elegant meal home.

DUCK BREAST WITH SUGAR SNAP PEAS AND MUSHROOMS

Serves 4

4 (6- to 8-ounce) duck breasts
Salt and freshly ground black pepper
4 garlic cloves, finely chopped
¾ pound sugar snap peas, ends trimmed

8 ounces mushrooms (cremini and button mushrooms preferred), thinly sliced
2 teaspoons sherry vinegar or red wine vinegar

1. Remove any silverskin from the duck breasts, and pat dry with a paper towel. If desired, score the duck skin approximately ½ inch apart in a crisscross pattern (be sure not to cut into the duck meat). Season both sides with the salt and pepper to taste.
2. Heat a large Lodge cast iron skillet over medium heat. Place the duck breasts in the hot skillet, fat side down, and sear until golden brown, 7 to 9 minutes. Turn the breasts over, and cook another 5 to 7 minutes. (The recommended serving temperature for duck is 145°F for medium rare.)
3. Transfer the breasts to a plate. Pour the rendered duck fat into a heatproof container; measure 1½ tablespoons of the rendered duck fat back into the skillet (refrigerate any remaining fat and keep for future use). Add the garlic, sugar snap peas, and mushrooms to the skillet. Season with the salt and pepper to taste. Add the vinegar, and cook, stirring, over medium heat until heated through, 5 to 7 minutes.
4. Cut the duck breasts into ½-inch-thick slices. Serve the duck with the vegetables on the side.

QUAIL AND DUMPLINGS

Serves 6

William Dissen, chef-owner of The Market Place restaurant in Asheville, North Carolina, uses wild game like quail on his menus. Preparing the velouté sauce in a cast iron Dutch oven allows for the development of rich, deep flavor when cooking the roux, as does pan searing the quail breasts in a cast iron skillet. French Perigord black truffles are now available in western North Carolina and add an earthy flavor to this unique interpretation of chicken and dumplings.

VELOUTÉ SAUCE

- 3 tablespoons unsalted butter
- 1 tablespoon olive oil
- ¼ cup diced (¼-inch) red onion
- ¼ cup diced (¼-inch) celery
- ¼ cup diced (¼-inch) carrot
- ¼ cup diced (¼-inch) fennel bulb
- 1½ tablespoons minced garlic
- ½ cup white wine
- ¼ cup all-purpose flour
- 1 quart chicken stock
- ¼ cup heavy cream
- 1 tablespoon hot sauce
- Kosher salt and freshly ground black pepper
- 1½ tablespoons finely chopped fresh flat-leaf parsley

DUMPLINGS

- 1½ quarts chicken stock
- 1 cup plus 2 tablespoons self-rising flour
- 1 tablespoon sliced fresh chives
- ½ teaspoon kosher salt
- ¼ teaspoon freshly ground black pepper
- ¼ cup buttermilk
- 1 large egg, beaten
- 2 tablespoons unsalted butter, melted and cooled

QUAIL

- 6 quail, cut into breasts and legs
- 2 tablespoons olive oil
- Kosher salt and freshly ground black pepper
- ¼ cup (½ stick) unsalted butter
- 4 sprigs fresh thyme
- 2 garlic cloves, peeled

GARNISHES

- 2 tablespoons thinly sliced fresh chives
- Aleppo pepper
- 1½ ounces black truffles (optional)

1. Prepare the Velouté Sauce: Heat the butter and oil together in a Lodge 5-quart cast iron Dutch oven over medium-high heat. When the butter begins to foam, add the onion, celery, carrot, and fennel, and cook, stirring, until translucent, 2 to 3 minutes. Stir in the garlic, and cook until aromatic. Add the wine, and scrape up any browned bits from the bottom of the pot. Continue to stir, and reduce the wine to a glaze, then sprinkle in the flour, and cook for about a minute, stirring, to create a roux. Whisk in the stock, and bring to a simmer over medium-high heat. Let cook for 15 to 20 minutes, then reduce the heat to medium, stir in the cream, and cook for another 5 minutes. Stir in the hot sauce, season with the salt and pepper to taste, and stir in the parsley. Taste and season as necessary. Keep warm.

2. Prepare the Dumplings: Bring the stock to a simmer in a large saucepan.

3. In a medium bowl, mix the flour, chives, salt, and pepper together. Form a well in the center, and add the buttermilk, beaten egg, and melted butter. Mix the flour into the wet ingredients. Add more buttermilk as necessary to yield a wet but stiff dough.

4. Working with 2 teaspoons, form the batter into oval dumplings the size of the teaspoon, adding them to the simmering stock as they are formed (you need 24 dumplings). Lightly poach the dumplings until they are firm, 6 to 8 minutes. Using a slotted spoon, remove the dumplings to a bowl, and cover with aluminum foil to keep warm.

5. Prepare the Quail: Place the quail legs in the still-simmering liquid used to poach the dumplings, and poach until cooked through, about 5 minutes. Remove from the liquid with a slotted spoon. When cool enough to handle, shred the meat from the bones. Reserve the meat, and discard the bones.

6. Heat the oil in a Lodge 15-inch cast iron skillet over medium-high heat until it begins to shimmer. Season the quail breasts with the salt and pepper to taste, and place, breast side down, in the hot pan. Cook the quail until golden, then turn over, reduce the heat to medium, and cook for 4 to 5 minutes.

7. Spoon the oil out of the skillet, then add the butter, thyme, and garlic. When the butter begins to foam, tilt the pan, and baste the quail with the butter until they are semifirm to the touch or an instant-read thermometer inserted into the thickest part of the breast registers 140°F.

8. For each serving, place a Lodge 5-inch square cast iron skillet on a folded white napkin on a serving plate. Place 4 dumplings in each skillet, and spoon about ½ cup of the Velouté Sauce over the dumplings. Sprinkle some of the shredded quail leg meat, sliced chives, and Aleppo pepper to taste over the sauce. Place a cooked quail breast in the center of the pan. If desired, shave 3 or 4 slices of the black truffle over the quail, and serve immediately.

❧ MEATS ❧

Lodge cast iron and tender, succulent meat is a marriage that's meant to be. The hot seasoned iron imparts savory flavor and that coveted perfect browning to each dish. Try George's Bean Hole Roast and Veggies, Pan-Fried Fajita Steaks, Center-Cut Bone-In Pork Chops with Apples and Chestnut Sauce, and the other stellar recipes here, and taste for yourself.

This recipe is from *Taste/Son of Best of Taste,* a collection of recipes from the "Taste" section of the newspaper that *The Minneapolis Star* published in 1974. It has always been a favorite of Eleanor Lodge Kellermann's family, served with cornbread. Eleanor is the great-granddaughter of company founder Joseph Lodge.

UPSIDE-DOWN MEATLOAF

Serves 4 to 6

Vegetable or olive oil
½ cup firmly packed light brown sugar
½ cup ketchup
1½ pounds ground beef
¾ cup crushed cracker crumbs

1 small onion, grated
¾ cup whole milk
2 large eggs, beaten
1½ teaspoons salt
¼ teaspoon black pepper
¼ teaspoon ground ginger

1. Preheat the oven to 350°F.
2. Grease a Lodge 10- x 5- x 3-inch cast iron loaf pan with the oil. Press the brown sugar evenly over the bottom, then evenly spread the ketchup over the sugar.
3. In a medium bowl, mix the remaining ingredients together, and shape into a loaf. Press firmly into the pan. Bake for 1 hour.
4. Remove from the oven. Let the meatloaf cool in the pan for 5 to 10 minutes. Turn the pan upside down onto a serving platter to unmold the loaf. Cut into slices to serve. Can be reheated.

A recipe passed down from his great-grandmother Dorothea Elizabeth Johnson, this is the first dish Kris Stubblefield learned how to make when he was growing up. Kris's wife, Masey, is the great-great-granddaughter of company founder Joseph Lodge.

BAKED SPAGHETTI

Serves 6

- 2 tablespoons olive oil
- 4 large garlic cloves, minced
- 2 large yellow onions, chopped
- 1½ teaspoons salt
- 2 pounds 80% lean ground beef
- 1 (28-ounce) can crushed tomatoes
- 1 (16-ounce) can tomato sauce
- 2 tablespoons balsamic vinegar or dry red wine
- 2 tablespoons sugar
- 1 tablespoon garlic powder
- 1 tablespoon dried basil
- 1 tablespoon dried tarragon
- 1 teaspoon red pepper flakes, or more to taste
- 16 ounces angel hair pasta
- Mozzarella cheese

1. Heat a Lodge 12-inch cast iron skillet over medium heat. Add the oil, garlic, onions, and ¼ teaspoon of the salt, and cook, stirring a few times, until the onions are softened, 8 to 10 minutes. Add the ground beef, and cook until no longer pink, breaking up any clumps of meat. Drain off any excess fat.

2. In a Lodge 5-quart cast iron Dutch oven, combine the tomatoes, tomato sauce, vinegar, sugar, garlic powder, basil, tarragon, red pepper, and remaining 1¼ teaspoons salt. Simmer over medium to medium-low heat for 10 to 15 minutes, then stir in the browned ground beef. Wipe out the skillet, and set aside.

3. Preheat the oven to 350°F.

4. Cook the pasta according to the package directions. Drain and pour the pasta into the skillet used to cook the beef. Pour the spaghetti sauce over the pasta. Shred the mozzarella as desired over the top, covering the sauce. Bake until the cheese is melted and starts to brown, 15 to 20 minutes.

DELTA-STYLE TAMALES

Makes 48 tamales

Mostly known for dishes like cornbread, greens, and fried catfish, the Mississippi Delta also has a rich history of serving up tamales. This regional staple gained its popularity when Latin immigrants moved to the area in the early 1900s. In this version from chef Tyler Brown, former executive chef of the Capitol Grille at The Hermitage Hotel in Nashville, he prepares his tamales with pasture-raised beef and uses coffee filters to wrap them instead of the traditional dried corn husks, a trick he picked up down South. Serve them with saltine crackers and hot sauce or with limes, salsa, and a dollop of sour cream.

5 pounds ground beef
¼ cup vegetable oil
1 medium onion, minced
¼ cup chili powder
2 tablespoons kosher salt
1 tablespoon onion powder
1 tablespoon garlic powder
2 teaspoons black pepper
1 teaspoon cayenne pepper
1 teaspoon ground cumin
8 cups self-rising white cornmeal mix
2 teaspoons kosher salt

1¾ cups lard
48 coffee filters
2 (32-ounce) cans tomato sauce
Hot sauce
1 medium onion, minced
3 jalapeño chiles, seeded and minced
2 tablespoons kosher salt
1 tablespoon onion powder
1 tablespoon garlic powder
2 teaspoons black pepper
1 teaspoon cayenne pepper
1 teaspoon ground cumin

1. Place the ground beef in a large, heavy stockpot. Cover with cold water. Bring to a boil over high heat. Cover the pot, reduce the heat to medium-low, and simmer until the meat is very tender, 2 to 2½ hours. Reserving the meat broth, drain the meat into a colander. Heat the oil in a Lodge 7-quart cast iron Dutch oven over medium heat. Stir in the onion, chili powder, salt, onion and garlic powders, black pepper, cayenne, and cumin until the onion is well coated with the spices. Add the meat, and stir to coat. Cook, stirring often, until the meat is hot, 7 to 10 minutes. Remove from the heat.
2. Combine the cornmeal mix, salt, and lard in a Lodge 5-quart cast iron Dutch oven, and mix well. Cook the dough over low heat for 10 minutes. Remove from the heat.
3. Lay a coffee filter on a clean work surface. Spread ¼ to ½ cup of the dough in an even layer across the center of the filter. Pat it out to your desired thickness in the form of a rectangle. Spoon 1 to 2 tablespoons of the filling in a line down the center of the dough. Holding opposite sides of the filter, roll the tamale so that the dough surrounds the filling and forms a narrow cylinder or package. Fold the top and bottom of the filter under to enclose the tamale. Tie the package closed crosswise with kitchen twine. Place the completed tamales in a single layer on a baking sheet. Repeat until all the dough and filling are used. Wash and dry the 7-quart Dutch oven. Arrange the tamale bundles in a single layer on the bottom of the Dutch oven.
4. In a large saucepan, combine the tomato sauce, 6 cups of the reserved meat broth, hot sauce to taste, onion, jalapeños, and next 6 ingredients. Bring to a boil, then carefully pour over the tamales. Cover the pot, and cook the tamales at a slow simmer for 3 to 4 hours. An instant-read thermometer inserted in the center of a tamale should register 180°F. To serve, remove the tamales from their coffee-filter jackets, and top with their simmering sauce.

⤙ BEAN HOLE COOKING ⤚

The description, directions, and recipe that follow (pages 118-120) for this technique of Dutch oven cookery were contributed by J. Wayne Fears. In his wide and varied career, he has been a wildlife specialist, developer and operator of hunting lodges in Alabama, and the editor-in-chief of *Rural Sportsman* and *Hunting Camp Journal* magazines. He is the author of more than 30 books on outdoor-related topics and is a columnist and contributor to numerous outdoor- and hunting-related periodicals. Visit him at jwaynefears.com.

A favorite method of cooking in hunting and fishing camps in the northeastern U.S., High Rockies, and Canada is what is commonly called "bean hole cooking." Bean hole cooking, according to historians, dates back for centuries to the early days of the Penobscot Indians of Maine. They found they could slow cook food by placing it in a hole dug in the earth that had been heated by building a fire in it. The food to be cooked was set in the hot coals, then the hole was covered with rocks and earth to seal in the heat. At the end of the day, they returned to a prepared meal.

Early settlers learned this method of cooking and added the cast iron pot as the vessel to hold the food. French voyagers carried this cooking technique into Canada, mountain men took it to the Rockies, and explorers took it to other parts of North America. Think of it as the early American version of the slow cooker.

It was in New England that the technique got its name "bean hole cooking." Back before stoves were common in logging camps, cooks did much of their cooking in cast iron Dutch ovens, often in holes in the ground, just like the Penobscot Indians. This was especially true of the cooks who followed the log drives down the rivers. Beans were the common table fare for these hardworking men, often three times a day. Because beans were the most common dish baked this way, the term "bean hole" cooking became the name used to describe the method.

For many years, I hunted and fished with Pam and Ken French at their log cabin camp in central Maine. Outside their cabin, down near the lakeshore, Ken built a permanent bean hole. Miss Pam would prep her tasty dishes, and Ken placed the loaded Lodge cast iron Dutch oven (or ovens) into the hot coals in the bean hole. A top was placed on the hole and it was covered with dirt. After a day of hunting or fishing, we returned, and the evening meal was hot and ready to eat.

MAKE YOUR OWN BEAN HOLE

Following Ken's instructions, I have built a permanent bean hole at my cabin. It's the center of attention anytime I'm cooking for a group of guests. Here is how you can build your own permanent bean hole.

1. Cut a clean 55-gallon steel drum and cut it in half. Save the lid and discard the upper half.

2. In a safe area, away from any flammable material, near your cabin or campsite, dig a hole a little deeper and wider than the half drum. Line the bottom and sides of the hole with firebricks.

3. Next, drill several small holes in the bottom of the drum to allow water to drain in the event water should ever get inside. Place about 3 inches of sand in the bottom of the drum to prevent it from burning out. Put the drum in the firebrick-lined hole. Fill in the spaces between the bricks and the drum with sand. Place the lid on top of the drum, and you have a permanent bean hole.

COOKING IN A BEAN HOLE

Go hiking or fishing for the day and return to a hot meal. As with most cooking techniques, it will take a few trials to get the method perfected, but it's fun and, once it's worked out, it'll become a favorite way to bake in your camp.

1. When you want to bake a pot of beans or any other dish, simply build a fire in the steel drum. Leave the top off and let the hole get hot.

2. Place a Lodge cast iron camp Dutch oven, with a tight-fitting flat lid, filled with beans, stew, a roast with veggies, or a cobbler into the bed of coals in the bean hole.

3. Place a shovel of hot coals on top of the Dutch oven lid. Put the cover on top of the drum, and cover with dirt or sand. This will keep the temperature even for a long period of time.

Try this recipe from wildlife specialist, editor, and author J. Wayne Fears on your next camping adventure or when you're entertaining at home and the weather is nice enough to eat outside. Start early in the morning so that by dinnertime you've got a hot pot of beef and vegetables awaiting.

GEORGE'S BEAN HOLE ROAST AND VEGGIES

Serves 8

Nonstick cooking spray
1 (3- to 4-pound) beef chuck roast
2 pounds small red or Yukon Gold potatoes, cut in half
1 pound carrots, cut into 2-inch pieces
1 large onion, cut into wedges

1 cup beef broth
2 tablespoons extra-virgin olive oil
2 teaspoons dried rosemary, crushed
1 teaspoon dried sage, crushed
Salt and freshly ground black pepper

1. Spray a Lodge 12-inch cast iron camp Dutch oven (an oven with a flat lid) with nonstick cooking spray. Place the roast in the Dutch oven, and arrange the potatoes, carrots, and onion wedges around it; pour the beef broth over the ingredients. Drizzle the oil evenly over the roast and vegetables; sprinkle with the rosemary, sage, and salt and pepper to taste.

2. Cover the entire coverless pot tightly with heavy-duty aluminum foil, allowing just enough give so the lid will fit snugly on top of the oven over the foil. Put the lid on, and cover the entire Dutch oven tightly with foil again.

3. Bury the Dutch oven in the hot coals of the bean hole; cover, and cook overnight or all day (see Cooking in a Bean Hole, page 119).

4. Remove the Dutch oven from the bean hole. Serve the roast and vegetables in individual serving bowls.

SHEPHERD'S PIE

Serves 8

FILLING

- 4 tablespoons extra-virgin olive oil
- 2 pounds chuck roast or other beef stew meat with the fat trimmed, cut into 1-inch cubes
- 1 large Vidalia onion, chopped
- 4 garlic cloves, minced
- 2 teaspoons salt, plus more to taste
- 1 teaspoon freshly ground black pepper
- 1 teaspoon red pepper flakes (optional)
- 1 cup beef broth
- 1 teaspoon dried oregano
- 1 teaspoon dried thyme
- 1 tablespoon chopped fresh flat-leaf parsley
- 4 large carrots, cut into 1-inch pieces, or 1½ cups baby carrots
- 1½ cups frozen green peas
- 1 cup chopped celery
- 2 tablespoons all-purpose flour
- 1 cup water

MASHED POTATO CRUST

- 2 pounds baking potatoes, peeled and cut into 1-inch cubes
- 4 quarts water
- 1 tablespoon salt
- 3 tablespoons salted butter
- ½ cup milk
- ½ cup half-and-half
- 1 teaspoon freshly ground black pepper

This recipe is from Paul Kelly, a network instructor for Pitney Bowes. An excellent cook and lifelong devotee of Lodge cast iron, Paul regularly prepares dishes for family and friends in his Senoia, Georgia, home. Shepherd's pie is usually made using ground beef, but preparing it with tender pot roast makes it irresistible.

1. Prepare the Filling: Preheat the oven to 325°F. Heat 2 tablespoons of the oil in a Lodge 5-quart cast iron Dutch oven over medium-high heat. Add the beef, half the onion, half the garlic, the salt, black pepper, and, if desired, red pepper to the pan, and cook until the beef is browned on all sides, about 5 minutes. Add the broth, oregano, thyme, and parsley. Cover the pan, and transfer to the oven; bake until the meat is fork-tender, about 2 hours.

2. Remove the meat and broth, and wipe the pan clean. Place the remaining 2 tablespoons oil in the pan, and heat over medium-high heat. Add the remaining onion and garlic, and cook, stirring often, 2 minutes. Add the carrots, peas, and celery, and cook, stirring often, 2 minutes.

3. Return the meat to the pan; stir, and add enough of the broth to cover. Season with salt to taste. Cook over medium heat, stirring for 5 minutes.

4. Place the flour in a cup, and slowly add the water, whisking until smooth; if any lumps form, strain the flour mixture through a sieve. Add the flour mixture to the pan, and stir well to blend.

5. Increase the oven temperature to 350°F.

6. Prepare the Mashed Potato Crust: Place the potatoes in a stockpot; add the water and salt, and bring to a boil. Cook until the potatoes are tender, about 10 minutes. Drain. While the potatoes are still hot, stir in the butter until it melts. Add the milk, half-and-half, and pepper; mash until smooth.

7. Spoon the potatoes over the filling in the Dutch oven. Bake on the center rack, uncovered, 30 minutes. Turn on the broiler, and broil until the potatoes are browned, about 5 minutes. Check often to prevent burning.

S-L-O-W BRAISED BEEF CHUCK ROAST

Serves 6 to 8

Beef chuck roast is a classic braising cut—and no cookware does it better than cast iron, says Wendy Taggart, who, with her husband, Jon, operates Burgundy Pasture Beef, their ranch and butcher market store located just south of Dallas/Fort Worth in Texas. Typically, cuts that are not naturally tender (but very flavorful, with their complexity of fat, connective tissue, and muscle) are the best braising cuts. It is the braising process that "tenderizes" the meat.

1 (3- to 4-pound) boneless or bone-in chuck roast
1 tablespoon dried herbes de Provence (or your favorite combination of dried herbs)
1 teaspoon coarse kosher or sea salt
½ teaspoon cracked black pepper
1 tablespoon olive, peanut, or grapeseed oil, or more as needed
1 cup chopped onion
2 garlic cloves, chopped
¾ cup chopped celery
1 bay leaf
2 to 3 leafy celery tops (optional)
½ cup red wine (optional)
2 tablespoons cold butter (optional)

1. Pat the roast dry with paper towels. In a small bowl, combine the herbes de Provence, salt, and pepper, then liberally apply the mixture to the roast—top, sides, and bottom—rubbing it in so it adheres. Preheat the oven to 200°F.

2. Heat a Lodge cast iron Dutch oven or skillet just big enough to fit the roast over medium-high heat. When the pan is hot, add the oil, and swirl to coat the bottom. Place the roast in the pan to brown. The heat should be high enough that the roast gives off a peppy "sizzle," but not so hot that the herb rub burns. Sear the roast until it has a rich brown crust on all sides, 5 to 8 minutes per side. Remove the roast to a platter.

3. If necessary, add a little more oil, then add the onion, garlic, and celery. Cook, stirring a few times, until the vegetables are softened, about 5 minutes. Spread the vegetables evenly over the bottom of the pan, and set the chuck roast over them. Add the bay leaf and celery tops, if desired. Place a tight-fitting lid over the pot (using parchment paper

How Wendy Braises Beef

   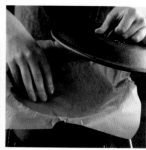

1. Season the beef before searing. Rub the seasoning mixture with your hands so the seasonings will adhere, covering all sides of the roast.

2. Select a pan with a lid that is closest in size to the cut you will braise. The lid needs to be heavy to prevent any moisture from escaping during the cooking process.

3. Sear the roast until a rich brown crust forms on all sides, and then cook at a very low temperature until tender.

4. If there is a lot of airspace in the pot, place a piece of parchment paper over the top of the pan, and push it down so it hangs about 1 to 2 inches above the meat. Set the lid on top of the parchment paper.

between the lid and pot, if desired, to prevent moisture from escaping), and braise in the oven until the roast is fork-tender, about 4 hours. The real test of doneness is that it tears apart easily with a fork. Transfer the roast to a serving platter, and cover with foil to keep it warm.

4. The finished roast will yield a wonderfully rich au jus in its purest form since no additional liquid was added. The key is the oven temperature—200°F—which allows the roast to produce its own juices during the slow braising process. You may serve the jus as is by pouring it back over the roast or serving it on the side with a ladle (discard the bay leaf and celery tops). Or you can reduce it over medium heat to strengthen the flavor; be sure to use a whisk to incorporate any tasty browned bits hanging onto the pan. Or you can make a red wine sauce from the jus—add the red wine, if desired, and boil over medium heat until reduced by about a third or more (taste test it for where you want it to be). Remove from the heat, and swirl in the cold butter (melting as you mix it), if desired. Season with salt and/or pepper to taste.

This panini tastes like a good steak dinner nestled between two slices of bread. It's even better when toasted on a cast iron grill pan. Cookbook author Sheri Castle advises that you keep a jar of the Onion Jam stashed in the fridge at all times. "It's habit forming, and you never know when a craving might strike."

ROAST BEEF, BLUE CHEESE, AND ONION JAM PANINI

Serves 6

- ½ cup crumbled blue cheese
- 1 tablespoon mayonnaise
- 1½ teaspoons prepared horseradish, or to taste
- 12 large ½-inch-thick slices country-style white bread
- 6 ounces thinly sliced high-quality roast beef
- 1 Granny Smith apple, unpeeled, cored, and sliced paper thin
- ¾ cup Onion Jam (recipe at right)
- 3 tablespoons salted butter, softened

1. In a small bowl, stir the blue cheese, mayonnaise, and horseradish together, mashing the cheese with a fork until the mixture is almost smooth. Store in the refrigerator, covered, for up to 3 days, if desired. Return to room temperature before using.

2. Place 6 slices of the bread on a work surface, and spread each with 1 heaping tablespoon of the blue cheese spread. Divide the roast beef and apple among the bread slices, covering each evenly. Spread about 1 tablespoon of the Onion Jam over the top of each. Set the remaining bread slices on top. Generously butter the tops and bottoms of the panini.

3. Heat a Lodge 12-inch cast iron grill pan over high heat. Working in batches, arrange the panini on the hot surface, and weigh down the top with a cast iron grill press or skillet or by pressing with a metal spatula. Toast, turning once, until the bread is browned, about 5 minutes per side. Serve warm with the remaining Onion Jam on the side.

ONION JAM

Makes about 2 cups

- 6 tablespoons (¾ stick) salted butter
- 2 pounds yellow onions, halved lengthwise and thinly sliced
- ¼ cup firmly packed light brown sugar
- ¼ cup red wine
- 1 tablespoon balsamic vinegar
- 2 teaspoons finely chopped fresh rosemary
- Kosher salt and freshly ground black pepper

1. Melt the butter in a Lodge 12-inch cast iron skillet over medium heat. Add the onions, and stir to coat. Cover the skillet, and cook, stirring occasionally, until the onions are completely limp, about 15 minutes.

2. Uncover the skillet, and reduce the heat to medium-low. Cook, stirring often to scrape up the brown glaze that forms on the bottom of the skillet, until the onions are very soft and golden brown, about 25 minutes more.

3. Add the brown sugar, wine, and vinegar. Stir until the sugar dissolves and the liquid cooks away, about 5 minutes.

4. Remove from the heat. Stir in the rosemary, and season with the salt and pepper to taste. Set aside to cool to room temperature. Store in the refrigerator, covered, for up to 1 week.

How Sheri Makes a Panini

1. Use a spread or some other type of condiment on the bread slices to help the sandwich hold together during cooking.

2. Use a heavy pan, like another cast iron skillet, to press down the sandwich when it's cooking on the grill pan.

3. Alternatively, you can use a metal spatula to press the sandwich, if desired.

4. Wait until the bread is nice and browned before turning—this will take about 5 minutes per side.

MARTY NATION'S SHORT RIBS

Serves 4 to 6

Jane Handel's bond with her brother, Marty, extends to a mutual love of good food prepared in cast iron pans, like his succulent recipe for short ribs—a favorite on cold nights.

5 pounds beef short ribs, cut into 2½-inch lengths
Salt and freshly ground black pepper
2 tablespoons canola or other vegetable oil that can withstand high temperature
1 cup chopped yellow onions
½ cup chopped carrots
¾ cup chopped celery
2 tablespoons tomato paste
2 tablespoons unbleached all-purpose flour
1 cup hearty red wine
1½ cups beef stock
6 medium russet or Yukon Gold potatoes, peeled and halved
3 to 4 medium yellow onions, quartered
4 large carrots, cut into 1½-inch pieces
½ pound green beans, trimmed and cut into 2-inch lengths, and/or 1 cup green peas

1. Preheat the oven to 375°F (or 400°F if you want the short ribs to cook faster).

2. Season the short ribs with the salt and pepper on both sides. Heat the oil in a Lodge 7-quart cast iron Dutch oven over high heat until very hot. In batches, add the short ribs in a single layer, and sear until golden brown on both sides. Remove the ribs from the pan, and pour off and discard all but 2 tablespoons of fat.

3. Add the chopped onions, carrots, and celery to the Dutch oven, and cook over low heat, stirring occasionally until tender and translucent, 15 to 20 minutes. Add the tomato paste, stir, and cook until reduced and darkened, about 4 minutes. Add the flour, and stir until fully combined with the vegetable mixture; cook another 3 to 4 minutes, stirring continuously.

4. Add the wine, scraping up any browned bits on the bottom of the pot. Reduce the wine over medium heat by three-quarters, then add the short ribs, pour the stock over the ribs, and simmer over low heat until the liquid is reduced again by three-quarters, about another 15 minutes. Place in the oven, and bake, uncovered, until the short ribs seem to be about 80 percent done, 1 to 1½ hours. Add the potatoes, quartered onions, and carrot pieces to the pot. Return to the oven, uncovered, and cook until the vegetables and short ribs are tender. Add the green beans and/or peas, and cook until they are tender, another 5 to 10 minutes.

5. Remove the pot from the oven. Transfer the meat (which should be so tender that it is falling off the bone) to the center of a large platter, and surround it with the vegetables. If the sauce seems too thin, reduce it over high heat on top of the stove. Another way to thicken it would be to puree the chopped vegetables in it using an immersion blender. Pour some of the reduced sauce over the meat on the platter, and serve the remainder in a pitcher at the table for anyone who desires extra sauce.

THE LIFE AND TIMES OF AN IRON PAN

Jane Handel

Writer, artist, editor, and co-publisher of **Edible Ojai**

In 2006, my brother, Marty Nation, competed in the First Annual BBQ'n at the Autry Barbecue Championship and Festival in Los Angeles. He brought along a family heirloom and special talisman—our late mother's oversized cast iron frying pan. This pan was her primary and favorite cooking equipment for many decades. It had cooked a lifetime of family meals, from Southern fried chicken to spaghetti sauce and just about everything else. It was the one thing of hers that Marty requested when she died, and it soon became a favorite cooking tool in his own kitchen.

Marty cooked with that big iron skillet throughout the Championship weekend. He even won first prize in the "Anything But Barbecue" category and credits our mother's pan with helping him to win against seasoned competitors from all over the country. Of course the pan played a significant role. But the fact that he's a graduate of the French Culinary Institute in New York and has cooked at some of New York City's top restaurants might also have contributed a soupçon to chef Marty's success.

Sadly, when he returned home after the competition, Marty discovered that his lucky pan had, rather mysteriously, developed a crack across the bottom. But instead of being thrown out, it soon became the namesake—Iron Pan—of a restaurant he opened in Ojai, California. Prominently displayed during the lifespan of the restaurant, the now-retired pan shared a place of honor next to his trophy from the contest. And when he wasn't behind the stove cooking, Marty would regale one and all with stories about his mother's now-legendary iron pan.

Over the years, Marty became a zealous collector of cast iron pans of every description, obsessively scouring flea markets and antiques stores for them on road trips far and wide. I, too, have my own trusty assortment that are used on a daily basis—whether I'm making pancakes on the iron griddle, a frittata in the iron skillet, or of course, spaghetti sauce adapted from our mother's recipe in the iron Dutch oven. I can't imagine cooking in anything else.

What worked for our mother continues to work for us. Like her, I've now had some of my iron pans for more than 40 years and suspect that my children and niece, Marty's daughter, will continue to cook with them when we're gone. For that matter, all of those trace elements of iron in our systems could mean that the iron pan legacy will continue well into the future as part of our family's DNA.

PAN-FRIED FAJITA STEAKS

Serves 4

Fajitas are a restaurant favorite, but John Meyer of Main Dish Media has started making them at home—and they've become a regular request when friends come over. He cooks the steaks and vegetables in cast iron skillets, and serves the fajitas straight out of the pans. "Unlike most fajita recipes, I use whole steaks, as well as big cuts of vegetables. If I wanted small slices and bites, I'd be doing stir-fry!" John explains. When left whole, the steaks develop a flavorful sear, while the whole vegetables retain their taste and texture.

2 tablespoons chili powder
1 tablespoon dried oregano
1 tablespoon ground cumin
2 teaspoons kosher salt, plus more to taste
2 teaspoons freshly ground black pepper, plus more to taste
4 (10- to 12-ounce) beef strip steaks
3 tablespoons vegetable oil
8 fajita-style flour tortillas
2 yellow bell peppers, cut in half and seeded
8 plum tomatoes, cut in half
12 green onions, trimmed
2 limes, cut in half

1. Preheat the oven to 350°F. Preheat 2 large Lodge cast iron skillets over medium-high heat.
2. Combine the chili powder, oregano, cumin, salt, and pepper in a small bowl; rub the mixture evenly over the steaks.
3. Pour 1 tablespoon of the oil into each of the hot skillets. Add 2 steaks to each pan, and sear, turning every minute, until the steaks reach the desired degree of doneness (10 to 12 minutes or an internal temperature of 120°F for medium rare). Transfer the steaks to a platter, cover loosely with foil, and let stand.
4. Wrap the tortillas in foil; warm in the oven as the vegetables cook.
5. Increase the heat under the skillets to high. Add some of the remaining 1 tablespoon oil to each pan, if necessary. Divide the bell peppers, tomatoes, green onions, and lime halves into 2 equal piles; add to the hot pans. Cook, tossing the vegetables and limes a few times, until slightly charred, 3 to 4 minutes. Transfer the mixture to the platter with the steaks.
6. To serve, heat both skillets over high heat; return the steaks and fajita vegetables to the pans, and squeeze the charred lime halves over the top. Serve with the warm tortillas. Each diner gets their own steak and can help themselves to the vegetables in the pans.

Thick, luscious veal chops are seared in a salted, hot, dry skillet after marinating in herbs. The fat on the chops helps them grill to perfection. Says cookbook author Ellen Wright, "The only pan I would ever use to make these chops is my favorite cast iron skillet, which I've had for 50 years. It's got a half-inch-tall side, so it's basically flat. To clean it, I run it under hot water when it's still warm, then wipe it off with a paper towel."

GRILLED VEAL CHOPS

Serves 6

1 tablespoon dried or fresh rosemary leaves

1 tablespoon dried or fresh thyme leaves

6 (1½-inch-thick) veal chops, trimmed of excess fat (don't remove all of it!)

1 to 2 tablespoons kosher salt

2 lemons, quartered

Watercress sprigs for garnish (optional)

1. Sprinkle the rosemary and thyme evenly on both sides of the chops, and keep at room temperature for about 2 hours.

2. Heat a Lodge 15-inch cast iron skillet over medium-high heat on the grill. Sprinkle the salt in the pan. Sear the chops until golden brown on each side and slightly pink inside, 4 to 5 minutes per side.

3. Remove the pan from the grill. Serve the chops as soon as possible with a wedge of lemon, and garnish with watercress, if desired.

For cooking instructor and food writer Jane Gaither, known in Tennessee as "Gourmet Gadget Gal," the secret to grilling restaurant-quality steaks at home means pulling out her Lodge grill pan, quickly searing the steaks on the stove, and finishing them in the oven. This recipe goes from stove-top to table in 10 minutes.

CAST IRON GRILLED STEAKS WITH BLUE CHEESE BUTTER

Serves 2

BLUE CHEESE BUTTER
- ½ cup (1 stick) unsalted butter, softened
- 1 (4-ounce) package crumbled blue cheese
- 1 teaspoon Worcestershire sauce
- Pinch of salt
- Freshly ground black pepper

STEAKS
- 2 (1-inch-thick) beef strip steaks
- 1 teaspoon vegetable oil
- Salt and freshly ground black pepper

1. Prepare the Blue Cheese Butter: Cream the butter in a small bowl, then add the blue cheese, Worcestershire, salt, and pepper, and beat until smooth. Using a 12-inch piece of plastic wrap, spoon out the butter mixture and roll it up like a log, twisting the ends. Freeze the butter until firm or for up to 1 month.

2. Preheat the oven to 350°F.

3. Prepare the Steaks: Bring the steaks to room temperature. Heat a Lodge grill pan over high heat until smoking hot. Carefully brush the pan with the oil.

4. Season the steaks on both sides with the salt and pepper to taste. Carefully place the steaks on the hot grill pan, and grill 2 minutes per side.

5. Transfer the grill pan to the oven, and bake for 2 minutes.

6. Remove the pan from the oven, and let the steaks stand 5 minutes. Serve with a pat of Blue Cheese Butter on each steak.

GARLIC-TOPPED FLANK STEAK ROULADE

Serves 4 to 6

- 2 pounds grass-fed flank steak
- Sea salt and freshly ground black pepper
- 4 strips pork bacon, cooked (but not crispy) and chopped
- 2 cups loosely packed organic spinach leaves, chopped
- ⅓ cup chopped organic sun-dried tomatoes
- 1 cup chopped organic button mushrooms (7 or 8 whole mushrooms)
- 2 tablespoons coconut oil
- 5 organic garlic cloves, minced

This elegant yet easy recipe comes from Tammy Credicott, best-selling author of *Make-Ahead Paleo*, *The Healthy Gluten-Free Life*, and *Paleo Indulgences*. And while this tasty flank steak may look challenging, the steps are quite simple and will leave your guests thinking you're a culinary rock star! You can find more delicious recipes on her website at thehealthygflife.com.

1. Preheat the oven to 425°F.

2. With a meat mallet or rolling pin, pound the flank steak to an even ⅓-inch thickness. This will give you more surface area to work with when stuffing it.

3. Season the steak with the salt and pepper on both sides, then lay it out flat in front of you. Sprinkle the chopped bacon over it in a single layer, then evenly layer on the spinach, tomatoes, and mushrooms, in that order. Roll the steak up lengthwise tightly into a log (roulade), then tie it with kitchen string in 2 or 3 places to hold it together. (At this point, you can wrap the roulade in plastic wrap and refrigerate overnight, if desired. Bring to room temperature before cooking.)

4. Heat the oil in a Lodge 12-inch cast iron skillet over medium-high heat. When the pan is really hot, sear the roulade until browned on all sides, 2 to 3 minutes total.

5. Remove the pan from the heat, and sprinkle the garlic all over the roulade. Place the skillet in the oven; bake until the stuffing is hot but the meat is still pink in the center, 10 to 15 minutes.

6. Remove from the oven, and let the roulade stand for 10 minutes. Remove the twine, slice into pinwheels, and serve.

How Tammy Makes a Roulade

1. Pounding the steak to an even ⅓ inch guarantees the steak will cook evenly. This step also tenderizes the steak to prevent it from being unpleasantly chewy.

2. Sprinkle the stuffing ingredients over the meat; leave a ½-inch border around the edge to keep the stuffing from spilling out when the steak is rolled up.

3. Roll the steak up lengthwise tightly into a log, then tie it with kitchen string in 2 or 3 places to hold it all together.

4. Make sure the pan is very hot before you place the roulade into the pan for searing so that each side gets nice and brown.

TOASTED CHILE-CUMIN MARINATED SKIRT STEAK TACOS

Serves 4

"I love to create marinades using toasted whole chiles and spices because they allow you to create richness and depth of flavor quickly," enthuses Norman King, a former *Southern Living* Test Kitchen professional. In this recipe, the marinade plays a dual role: imparting both flavor and tenderness to the meat. Plus, cooking it without wiping off the excess marinade gives the steak its own sauce. After the steak stands, simply slice and serve. "No hot sauce required," says Norman.

- 3 dried guajillo chiles (see Kitchen Note)
- 1 cup boiling water
- 2 tablespoons olive oil
- ½ cup chopped sweet onion
- 2 garlic cloves, peeled
- ½ teaspoon cumin seeds
- ½ teaspoon dried oregano
- 2½ teaspoons kosher salt
- 1 tablespoon cider vinegar
- 1½ pounds skirt steak, trimmed of fat
- Radish-Tomatillo Salad (recipe at right)
- 8 to 10 (6-inch) fajita-size corn tortillas
- 1 tablespoon vegetable oil
- Crumbled queso fresco

1. Heat a Lodge 12-inch cast iron skillet over medium heat until hot, about 5 minutes. Add the chiles, and toast, turning often, until they puff and become fragrant, 1 to 2 minutes. (Chiles burn quickly, so keep a watchful eye.) Cut the chiles open with kitchen shears; remove the seeds. Cut off the stems. Place the chiles in a heatproof medium bowl, and cover with the boiling water. Let stand 10 minutes.

2. Meanwhile, heat the olive oil in the same skillet over medium heat. Add the onion, garlic, cumin seeds, and oregano, and cook, stirring, until the onion is just tender, 2 to 3 minutes. Let cool 5 minutes. Add the onion mixture, salt, and vinegar to the chiles and their soaking water, and process in a blender or food processor until smooth. Cover and chill 30 minutes. Wash and dry the skillet.

3. Pour the chile mixture over the steak in a shallow dish, cover, and chill 2 to 4 hours.

4. Make the Radish-Tomatillo Salad.

5. Lightly brush the tortillas with the vegetable oil on both sides. Heat the same cast iron skillet over medium heat. Once hot, cook the tortillas one at time until slightly charred, 1 to 2 minutes per side. Wrap in aluminum foil, and keep warm.

6. Heat the same skillet over medium heat. Remove the steak from the marinade, discarding the marinade; don't wipe off any of the clinging marinade. Cook the steak in the hot skillet to your desired degree of doneness, 7 to 8 minutes per side for medium.

7. Remove the steak to a cutting board. Let stand 5 to 10 minutes before slicing against the grain into thin strips. Serve in the charred tortillas with Radish-Tomatillo Salad and queso fresco.

KITCHEN NOTE:

Dried chiles are easily found in the ethnic or Latin sections of local supermarkets. They are commonly sold in small cellophane bags and are nestled next to dried herbs and spices in similar packaging. If guajillo chiles are not available, feel free to substitute the same amount of New Mexico chiles.

RADISH-TOMATILLO SALAD

Makes about 2 cups

- 1 cup radishes, cut into thin strips
- 1 medium tomatillo, husked and diced, or green tomato, diced
- 1 small Kirby cucumber, halved lengthwise and thinly sliced
- 1½ teaspoons kosher salt
- ¼ teaspoon sugar
- ½ cup chopped fresh cilantro
- ¼ cup chopped fresh mint
- 1 tablespoon fresh lime juice

1. In a medium bowl, toss together the radishes, tomatillo, cucumber, salt, and sugar. Transfer the mixture to a colander, and let stand 30 minutes.

2. Transfer the mixture back to the bowl, and stir in the cilantro, mint, and lime juice just before serving.

This dish creates an awful lot of smoke, so chef Patrick Reilly of the Majestic Grille in Memphis likes to cook it outside on the burner of his gas grill. "You can also use the burner of an outdoor fryer," says Patrick.

SEARED ROSEMARY AND GARLIC PORTERHOUSE WITH BROWNED BUTTER

Serves 2

- 1 fresh rosemary sprig
- 1 garlic clove, sliced
- ¼ cup extra-virgin olive oil
- 1 (2-pound) Porterhouse steak (dry-aged Prime is always best but good Choice will also work)

- Kosher salt and freshly ground black pepper
- ¼ cup (½ stick) unsalted butter
- 1 tablespoon chopped fresh curly parsley

1. Let the rosemary and garlic infuse in the oil for a few hours.
2. Take the steak out of the refrigerator 1 hour before you plan to cook it, and allow it to come to room temperature.
3. Place a large Lodge cast iron skillet on the gas eye of one of the burners of a gas grill set on high, and leave it for at least 20 minutes. (Patrick finds it best to go make a gin and tonic or a martini to pass the time.)
4. Using the rosemary sprig as a brush, cover the steak with the infused oil. Sprinkle with the salt and pepper to taste. Place the steak in the hot skillet over high heat. Let cook (without moving) for about 3 minutes.
5. Using tongs, lift the steak out of the skillet, and pour the drippings from the skillet into a heatproof container. (Use a grill mitt to grab the skillet handle—it's going to be incredibly hot.) Return the pan to the burner; place the steak, uncooked side down, back in the skillet, and cook for 2 to 3 minutes.
6. Remove the steak to a cutting board. Let stand for 5 to 6 minutes to allow the juices to settle. Using a sharp knife, carve the meat off the bone, then slice lengthwise and place on a platter.
7. Wipe the skillet clean, and add the butter. Reduce the heat to medium, and cook until the butter is foamy and brown. Stir in the parsley, and pour the butter mixture over the sliced steak. Serve immediately.

"This beautiful recipe," says Masey Lodge Stubblefield, great-great-granddaughter of company founder Joseph Lodge and daughter of current Lodge president, Henry Lodge, and wife, Donna, "was born out of a Friday night in which junk food cravings were high, and spring was in full force. It blew us away with its smoky, crispy crust topped with a variety of hot and cold fresh veggies and greens."

GRILLED PIZZA

Makes one 14-inch pizza; Serves 4

- 6 plum tomatoes, skewered and charred on the grill, about 5 minutes per side
- 3 garlic cloves, minced
- Salt and black pepper
- 1 red onion, sliced
- Shiitake mushrooms, stems discarded
- ½ pound Italian sausage, casings removed
- 1 pound refrigerated pizza dough
- 2 tablespoons olive oil
- Fresh mozzarella cheese, thinly sliced, cut into small pieces, or shredded
- Chopped fresh basil or baby arugula mixed with a dash of olive oil, salt, and fresh lemon juice

1. In a medium bowl, combine the grilled tomatoes, garlic, and salt and pepper to taste, mixing and crushing the tomatoes into a sauce. Set aside.

2. Preheat the grill to medium high. Grill the onion and mushrooms directly on the grill or using a Lodge Reversible Pro-Grid Iron Griddle. As you finish grilling them, transfer to a Lodge 9-ounce cast iron oval mini server on the top rack of the grill to keep warm. Meanwhile, cook the sausage in a Lodge 8-inch cast iron skillet on the side of the grill or attached burner until no longer pink, breaking into small pieces.

3. Lightly flour a work surface and the pizza dough; roll it out ½ inch thick, trimming off any excess. (Masey recommends brushing any dough trimmings with oil and garlic powder and popping them in the toaster oven for about 5 minutes on 350°F for a delightful snack/appetizer.) Brush one side of the dough with some of the oil, and place on a Lodge 14-inch cast iron round baking pan, oil side down, and grill for 2 to 3 minutes.

4. Remove the pan from the grill, brush the top side of the dough with oil, and flip it over. Top the grilled side of the dough with the tomato sauce, then scatter your choice of the grilled toppings and sausage over the top. Finally, cover with the mozzarella. Place the pan back on the grill, close the lid, and cook for 4 to 5 minutes. If the mozzarella hasn't melted, remove the pizza from the grill, and stick under the broiler for another few minutes to melt.

5. Top with the basil or dressed arugula, and serve.

This comforting dish of sausage, potatoes, onions, and red roasted peppers from Chuck Aflitto, TV personality and chef, bakes up in just a half hour. The aromas are intriguing, the taste sweet and spicy all at once, and the potatoes crispy and delicious.

BAKED SAUSAGE AND POTATOES WITH ROASTED RED PEPPERS

Serves 6 to 8

- 3 tablespoons salted butter
- 2 tablespoons extra-virgin olive oil
- 2 large onions, thinly sliced
- 4 russet potatoes, peeled and thinly sliced
- 2 hot sausage links, casings removed
- ½ (8-ounce) jar roasted red peppers, drained
- ¼ cup grated Parmigiano-Reggiano cheese
- Sea salt and freshly ground black pepper

1. Preheat the oven to 450°F. Grease a Lodge 36-ounce cast iron oval serving dish with 1 tablespoon of the butter.

2. Melt the remaining 2 tablespoons butter with 1 tablespoon of the oil in a Lodge 10-inch cast iron skillet over medium heat. Add the onions, and cook, stirring occasionally, until golden brown, about 20 minutes. Remove from the heat.

3. Layer the potato slices evenly over the bottom and up the side of the oval server, overlapping them; reserve enough of the potato slices to cover the top. Crumble the sausage meat over the potatoes. Arrange the sautéed onions evenly over the sausage, then the roasted peppers. Arrange the remaining potatoes over the peppers, drizzle with the remaining 1 tablespoon oil, sprinkle with the cheese, and season with the salt and pepper to taste.

4. Bake until the potatoes are browned, the sausage is fully cooked, and you can easily insert a sharp knife through the center, about 25 minutes.

This recipe is from Francine Maroukian, an award-winning food writer and contributing editor to *Garden & Gun, Travel + Leisure,* and *Esquire* magazines. "Be sure to make this with small, firm squash," she advises. "Larger squash hold so much water that you'll get steamed rather than browned vegetables."

PAN PORK WITH RAPID RATATOUILLE

Serves 4

1 (2½-pound) boneless pork loin
Salt and freshly ground black pepper
2 tablespoons canola oil
2 tablespoons unsalted butter
1 shallot, minced

2 garlic cloves, minced
4 cups diced mixed pattypan squash and zucchini
1 cup diced tomatoes
Big pinch of torn fresh herbs (like basil, parsley, or thyme)

1. Preheat the oven to 375°F.

2. Season the pork loin with the salt and pepper to taste.

3. Heat a Lodge cast iron skillet over medium heat until hot. Add the oil, and sear the pork loin on all sides. Transfer the skillet to the oven, and roast until a meat thermometer inserted into the thickest portion registers 155°F and the pork is cooked through but still juicy, about 25 minutes. Transfer the pork to a cutting board to stand.

4. Return the skillet to medium heat. Add the butter, and let it melt, stirring frequently to scrape up any browned bits. When the butter is foaming slightly, add the shallot and garlic, stirring quickly to soften. As soon as they release their fragrances (about 1½ minutes), add the squash mix, and stir to coat with the flavored butter. Cook, stirring occasionally, until golden brown, about 6 minutes. Add the tomatoes and herbs; stir only once or twice to soften the tomatoes and release the aroma of the herbs.

5. Slice the pork loin, and place on 4 plates. Spoon the ratatouille onto the pork slices, adding the salt and pepper to taste, if desired.

CENTER-CUT BONE-IN PORK CHOPS WITH APPLES AND CHESTNUT SAUCE

Serves 2

"The secret to these chops is the searing they get on a cast iron griddle," declares Karen Cassady, coordinator of the Central Market Cooking Schools in Texas. The rich, deep flavors of the chestnut puree and the bright, spicy notes of the ichimi togarashi complement the classic combination of apples and pork. "I was introduced to this Japanese powdered red pepper by Tre Wilcox, a chef and *Top Chef* contender from Dallas who teaches in our cooking schools," says Karen.

KITCHEN NOTE:

Ichimi togarashi is a Japanese powdered red pepper available in specialty grocery stores and Asian markets. You can substitute freshly ground red pepper flakes.

2 slices apple-smoked bacon, finely chopped

1 tablespoon finely chopped shallot

1 medium Rome apple, peeled, cored, and chopped medium fine

2 bone-in center-cut pork chops (about 1 inch thick)

Fine sea salt to taste (about 1 teaspoon)

Ichimi togarashi (red pepper) to taste (about ¼ teaspoon; see Kitchen Note)

3 fresh sage leaves, finely chopped

2 tablespoons canned chestnut puree

4 tablespoons heavy cream

1 teaspoon chestnut honey or other full-flavored honey

1. Preheat the oven to 350°F.

2. Heat a Lodge 10½-inch cast iron griddle over medium heat until the pan is hot. Add the bacon; cook, stirring occasionally, until it has rendered some fat and begins to crisp. Add the shallot and apple, and cook, stirring occasionally, until the apple begins to soften, about 3 minutes.

3. While the apples cook, dust the chops with the sea salt, red pepper, and half of the sage.

4. Using a slotted spoon, transfer the apple mixture to a heatproof bowl, leaving as much liquid behind on the griddle as possible (there won't be much). Toss the remaining sage with the mixture in the bowl.

5. Over medium heat, sear the chops on the griddle in the liquid until browned, 1 to 2 minutes per side. Return the apple mixture to the griddle, surrounding the chops with it. Place the griddle in the oven, and bake until the chops register 160°F when an instant-read thermometer is inserted at the thickest point.

6. While the chops are in the oven, place the chestnut puree, 2 tablespoons of the cream, and the honey in a small bowl. Using a fork, mix to combine thoroughly.

7. When the chops are ready, remove the griddle from the oven, and transfer the chops and apple mixture to a tray. Place the griddle over medium heat, and scrape up any browned bits from the surface. Add the remaining 2 tablespoons cream, and stir with a whisk to incorporate the pan scrapings into the cream. Add the chestnut mixture and, stirring quickly, incorporate the cream with the pan scrapings into that mixture. This will form a thin sauce.

8. Pour a pool of the sauce on two warm dinner plates. Arrange the chops on the sauce, and top with the apple mixture. Enjoy!

"You can order this 'Pad-kee-mow' everywhere in Thailand as well as in most Thai restaurants in the U.S.," says St. Louis, Missouri-based cookbook author and cooking school teacher Naam Pruitt. "It's part of the Thai lunch repertoire. 'Kee-mow' translates into 'drunken' in English, but there is no alcohol in this dish," explains Naam. "Instead, because of its extreme spiciness, it's supposed to sober you up!"

DRUNKEN RICE NOODLES WITH PORK

Serves 2 to 4

- ½ (14-ounce) package dried medium rice noodles
- ¼ cup canola oil
- 4 garlic cloves, chopped
- 2 Thai chiles (see Kitchen Note), chopped
- 2 boneless pork chops (about 1 pound), trimmed of fat, thinly sliced, and marinated in 2 teaspoons soy sauce for 5 minutes
- 2 tablespoons sweet soy sauce
- 2 tablespoons soy sauce
- 1 tablespoon Thai fish sauce
- 1 tablespoon oyster sauce
- 2 tablespoons sugar
- 1 teaspoon ground white pepper
- ½ cup water, or as needed
- 1 red bell pepper, seeded and cut into thin strips
- 1 cup snow peas, trimmed and cut in half on a diagonal
- 1 cup fresh Thai basil leaves

1. Soak the noodles in warm water to cover for 20 minutes, then drain off the water, and set aside.

2. Heat a Lodge 14-inch cast iron wok over medium-high heat until hot. Add the oil, and wait until it is hot. Add the garlic and chiles; using a wide metal spatula, stir around until the mixture is fragrant and the garlic starts to turn color, about 1 minute.

3. Add the pork, and stir until cooked through. Add the drained noodles, both soy sauces, fish sauce, oyster sauce, sugar, white pepper, and water, and cook until the noodles are almost soft, stirring constantly, 5 to 8 minutes.

4. Stir in the pepper strips and snow peas, and cook until tender-crisp and the noodles are soft, just a few minutes. Turn off the heat. Stir in the basil, and serve.

KITCHEN NOTE:

Thai chiles have a lingering heat. They have an elongated, pointed shape and are 1 to 1½ inches long, with a thin skin and copious seeds. On a heat scale of 1 to 10, they clock in at 8.

A COOKING SECRET FROM NAAM

Soy sauce varies a great deal from brand to brand and country to country. I prefer to use Thai sweet soy sauce, which has a thick consistency and the flavor of molasses, with a subtle hint of soy. It is used to add sweetness and a dark color to a dish.

This is a favorite dish of Jennifer Brush, owner of The Pastry Brush bakery in Chardon, Ohio, and her husband, Andrew. They especially enjoy making it when they go camping, because the meat can be grilled briefly first to develop a crust and then cooked over a low fire or on a grill in a covered pot. It goes well with egg noodles or mashed potatoes, and Jennifer and Andrew like to serve it with homemade biscuits and coleslaw.

SPICED BRAISED PORK SHOULDER

Serves 4 to 6

SPICE RUB

- 2 tablespoons sugar
- 2 teaspoons kosher salt
- ½ teaspoon ground coriander
- ½ teaspoon ground cumin
- ½ teaspoon freshly ground black pepper
- ½ teaspoon ground cinnamon
- ½ teaspoon ground cardamom

BRAISED PORK

- 1 (3- to 4-pound) pork shoulder
- 3 tablespoons vegetable oil
- 1 bottle lager beer (avoid using a hoppy beer like an IPA)

GRAVY

- All-purpose flour as needed
- 2 teaspoons cider vinegar
- ¼ cup chopped fresh cilantro

1. Prepare the Spice Rub: Pour all the ingredients into a 1-gallon zip-top plastic bag, seal, and shake. Dry the pork shoulder with a paper towel, and place it in the bag. Rub the dry ingredients into the meat until they are nearly all adhered to the meat and all of the surfaces of the meat are covered. Squeeze the air out of the bag, seal, and refrigerate for 24 hours.

2. Prepare the Braised Pork: Preheat the oven to 225°F. Heat the oil in a Lodge 7-quart cast iron Dutch oven over medium-high heat until it sizzles. Brown all sides and edges of the pork shoulder. Pour in enough beer to cover the bottom of the pot—about ⅜ inch deep—no more! Bring the beer to a boil. Cover the pot, and place in the oven. Bake until the meat shreds easily with a fork, 3 to 4 hours.

3. Prepare the Gravy: Remove the meat from the pot, and wrap in aluminum foil. Pour the liquid from the pot into a heatproof measuring cup. Measure 1 tablespoon flour per cup of liquid, and place in the Dutch oven. Over low heat, add the braising liquid very slowly to the pot, whisking thoroughly to eliminate lumps, until all the liquid is added and the gravy is smooth. Turn the heat to high, and bring the gravy to a boil to thicken. Remove from the heat. Whisk in the vinegar and cilantro. Shred the meat using two forks, and discard any fatty pieces. Mix the shredded meat with the sauce in the pot, and serve.

SMOKED HAM HOCKS WITH HOPPIN' JOHN AND CARAMELIZED ONION JUS

Serves 6 to 8

Stephen Stryjewski, chef/co-owner of Cochon in New Orleans, has had ham hocks on the menu since the restaurant opened. "It's an underappreciated cut of meat that lacks versatility but packs incredible flavor," says Stephen. Making the multiple components of this dish requires a good bit of time, but it is worth the effort. For the hocks, choose large pork knuckles from the front legs above the first joint. They can have the skin on or off. "I like the texture of the slow-cooked skin, although hocks with the skin still on are hard to come by."

- 2 cups kosher salt
- 1 cup sugar
- 1 teaspoon curing salt (see Kitchen Note)
- 2 tablespoons juniper berries
- 2 tablespoons allspice berries
- 2 tablespoons fennel seeds
- 5 star anise
- ½ cup coriander seeds
- 10 bay leaves
- 8 garlic cloves, peeled
- 5 sprigs fresh thyme
- 2 sprigs fresh rosemary
- ½ cup black peppercorns
- 8 cups (2 quarts) water
- 1 gallon ice cubes
- 6 unsmoked ham hocks (2 to 3 pounds each)
- Caramelized Onion Jus (recipe follows)
- Hoppin' John (recipe at right)

1. To make the brine, stir the salt, sugar, herbs, garlic, and spices together in a large stockpot. Add the water, bring to a boil, and let simmer, stirring, until the salt and sugar are dissolved. Remove from the heat. Pour the ice in to cool.

2. Add the ham hocks to the cooled brine, adding additional water if needed to cover. Cover the stockpot, and refrigerate for 4 days.

3. Remove the hocks from the brine, and pat dry. Place the hocks on a wire rack set on a large baking sheet in the refrigerator, uncovered, for 24 hours to develop a sticky film to which the smoke can adhere.

4. In a smoker or using a charcoal or gas grill, smoke the hocks over indirect heat at 225°F until the meat falls off the bone with light pressure, about 6 hours.

5. While the hocks smoke, make the Caramelized Onion Jus and Hoppin' John.

6. To serve, place a scoop of the Hoppin' John in the center of a Lodge cast iron round mini server or a deep dish, and top with a ham hock. Top with ¼ cup of the caramelized onions, and serve.

KITCHEN NOTE:
Curing salt will give the hocks the nice rosy red color. Look for it online at sausagemaker.com; you'll want their Insta Cure #1 for this.

CARAMELIZED ONION JUS

Makes about 4 cups

- 2 tablespoons lard
- 3 quarts thinly sliced onions (3 to 4 large onions)
- ½ cup thinly sliced garlic (about 12 cloves)
- 2 tablespoons fresh thyme leaves
- ½ cup balsamic vinegar
- 1 quart pork stock, roasted chicken stock, or good-quality reduced-sodium beef stock
- Kosher salt
- Fresh lemon juice

1. Melt the lard in a Lodge 7-quart cast iron Dutch oven over high heat. Add the onions, reduce the heat to low, and cook, stirring frequently and allowing onions to caramelize slowly and turn golden. This will take about an hour.

2. Add the garlic, and let it become golden brown slowly, about 10 minutes, stirring often. Add the thyme, and deglaze with the vinegar. Reduce the liquid by half, and add the stock. Bring to a simmer, and continue to simmer, uncovered, until the liquid reduces by one-quarter to one-third and the jus is thick without being tacky, about 20 minutes. Season with the salt and lemon juice to taste, if desired.

HOPPIN' JOHN

Makes about 4 cups

- ½ pound dried black-eyed peas, rinsed and picked over
- ⅓ pound tasso or country ham, diced
- 5½ cups water
- 1 medium onion, cut in half, one half diced
- 2 garlic cloves, peeled
- 1 bay leaf
- ¼ pound bacon, cut into small pieces
- ½ large green bell pepper, seeded and diced
- 2 celery ribs, cut into small pieces
- ½ jalapeño chile, seeded and minced
- ½ teaspoon fresh thyme leaves
- ¾ cup raw brown jasmine rice
- 3 green onions, thinly sliced
- Leaves from ½ bunch fresh flat-leaf parsley, chopped
- 1 teaspoon kosher salt
- 1 teaspoon freshly ground black pepper

1. In a Lodge 7-quart cast iron Dutch oven, combine the black-eyed peas, tasso, and 4 cups of the water. Add the onion half, garlic, and bay leaf. Bring to a boil over high heat, reduce the heat to medium-low, and simmer gently until the peas are tender but not mushy, 2 to 2½ hours. Drain the peas, reserving the cooking liquid. Remove and discard the onion, garlic, and bay leaf from the peas. Transfer the peas to a bowl, and wipe out the Dutch oven.

2. Add the bacon to the pot, and render over medium-high heat until golden, stirring frequently. Add the diced onion, bell pepper, celery, and jalapeño, and cook, stirring a few times, until the onion is translucent, about 10 minutes. Add the thyme and remaining 1½ cups water to the pot, and bring to a boil. Add the rice, cover, reduce the heat to a simmer, and cook until the rice is tender, 17 to 22 minutes.

3. Stir the green onions, parsley, and black-eyed peas gently into the rice (you don't want to break the grains), season with the salt and pepper, and adjust the consistency with a bit of the reserved bean cooking liquid, if desired. Keep warm until ready to serve.

A well-kept secret of California wine country is the outstanding and abundant lamb produced there. Mint is a classic pairing with lamb, but this recipe also includes garlic. For those who find classic mint jelly overwhelming, the combination of fresh mint and garlic provides a welcome and light alternative. Completing his twist on the traditional dish, Al Hernandez, the food and wine editor for *The Vine Times*, also uses cauliflower as an alternative to mashed potatoes.

LAMB CHOPS WITH CAULIFLOWER "MASHED POTATOES"

Serves 4

12 (1- to 1½-inch-thick) lamb loin chops	¼ cup balsamic vinegar
½ teaspoon kosher salt, plus more to taste	¼ cup plus 1 tablespoon olive oil
½ cup tightly packed fresh mint leaves, finely chopped	1 head cauliflower, cut into small florets
1 tablespoon finely chopped garlic	1 tablespoon unsalted butter
	½ cup heavy cream
	Freshly ground black pepper

1. Season the lamb chops on both sides with salt; set aside.

2. In a small bowl, mix the mint, garlic, vinegar, and ½ teaspoon salt together. Add ¼ cup of the oil in a slow, steady stream, whisking constantly, until it thickens into an emulsion. Add the salt for taste. Set aside.

3. Bring ¼ to ½ inch water to a boil in a covered medium saucepan over medium heat. Place the florets in a steamer basket, set in the saucepan, cover, and steam until the cauliflower is tender, 8 to 10 minutes.

4. While the cauliflower steams, heat the remaining 1 tablespoon oil in a Lodge 15-inch cast iron skillet over medium-high heat about 1 minute. Add the lamb chops (you may need to cook them in batches), and cook 2 to 5 minutes per side, depending on their thickness and your desired degree of doneness (2 to 3 minutes per side for rare and 5 minutes plus for medium to medium-well). Remove to a plate, cover with aluminum foil, and let stand while you finish the cauliflower.

5. Remove the steamer basket from the saucepan, and discard the steaming water. Melt the butter in the pan, add the florets, and mash as you would for mashed potatoes. (For a smoother consistency, use a blender or food processor.) Add the cream, and heat through over low heat, 2 to 3 minutes. Season with the salt and pepper to taste.

6. To serve, spoon the cauliflower mash in the center of each plate, surround with 3 lamb chops, and spoon the sauce over each chop.

FISH & SHELLFISH

Whether you prefer oysters, salmon, catfish,
shrimp or other fish and seafood, with
recipes such as Pan-Seared Salmon with Dill
Sauce and Sautéed Asparagus, Trout Cakes
and Watercress Salad with Basil Vinaigrette,
and Lemongrass Shrimp, there's
a dish here you'll love.

"My grandparents on my father's side, Priscilla Bacon Millhiser and Frederick Millhiser, enjoyed vacationing on the Eastern Shore of Maryland and Delaware, with its abundant regional seafood and white beaches," remembers William Prescott Millhiser, member of the Lodge Board of Directors and great-great-grandson of company founder Joseph Lodge. "They would rent a cottage, and their sons and families would come to visit. Great fun was had by all. Grandpa would fish in the surf; his grandsons would play in the waves."

BAY COUNTRY OYSTERS AND FISH

Serves 4

- ¼ cup (½ stick) margarine or salted butter
- 1 cup finely chopped onion
- 1 pound flounder fillets, each cut into 4 pieces
- 1 (4-ounce) can sliced mushrooms, drained and juice reserved
- ½ pint (8 ounces) shucked oysters, drained and liquid reserved
- ½ cup liquid (combination of juice and liquid from mushrooms and oysters)
- ¼ cup dry sherry
- ½ teaspoon salt
- ⅛ teaspoon black pepper
- Hot cooked white or wild rice

1. Melt the margarine in a Lodge 12-inch cast iron skillet over medium heat. Add the onion, and cook, stirring, until glazed, 8 to 10 minutes.
2. Spread the onion evenly in the skillet. Lay the fish fillets over the onion. Spread the mushrooms over the fish. In a small bowl, combine the mushroom and oyster liquid, sherry, salt, and pepper. Pour over the fish and mushrooms. Cover and simmer over medium heat until the fish flakes easily when tested with a fork, 5 to 8 minutes.
3. Add the oysters to the skillet, and simmer, uncovered, basting frequently with the pan juices, until the edges of the oysters curl, about 5 minutes. Serve in a bowl over rice.

The Sacramento River is California's largest river and boasts runs of king, steelhead, and other types of salmon. The flavor and color of freshly caught wild salmon make for a luxurious and healthy meal. This fish is perfectly paired with another local favorite, asparagus. Areas around Sacramento are known for their asparagus production, and California is one of the nation's leading producers. This recipe is from Al Hernandez, the food and wine editor of *The Vine Times*.

PAN-SEARED SALMON WITH DILL SAUCE AND SAUTÉED ASPARAGUS

Serves 4

4 (4- to 6-ounce) skin-on salmon fillets
Kosher salt
2 pounds asparagus (preferably thin or medium-thick)
1 tablespoon plus 2 teaspoons olive or grapeseed oil
½ cup crème fraîche or sour cream
2 tablespoons finely chopped fresh dill
1 teaspoon granulated garlic
Freshly ground black pepper

1. Season the salmon fillets liberally with the salt; set aside.
2. Take one spear of the asparagus and, using both hands, one at each end of the spear, break it in two. It will naturally break at the right spot. Then cut the rest of the spears using the broken one as a guide. Discard the woody ends.
3. Heat 1 tablespoon of the oil in a Lodge 12-inch cast iron skillet over high heat until hot. Place the salmon, skin side down, in the pan. After about 1 minute, reduce the heat to medium. Cook the fillets another 5 to 8 minutes, depending on their thickness.
4. While the salmon cooks, whisk together the crème fraîche, dill, and granulated garlic in a small bowl until smooth. Season with the salt and pepper to taste. Set aside.
5. Turn the fillets over, and cook to medium or medium-well doneness, whichever you prefer, another 3 to 5 minutes. Transfer to a plate, cover with aluminum foil, and let stand for 10 minutes.
6. To the same skillet, still over medium heat, add the remaining 2 teaspoons oil and the asparagus spears, season with the salt, and cook, stirring occasionally, until the asparagus spears are tender, 7 to 10 minutes.
7. To serve, arrange the asparagus in the center of each plate, set a salmon fillet, skin side down, on top, and spoon the dill sauce over the salmon.

This recipe is from George B. Stevenson, former chef de cuisine at Pearl's Foggy Mountain Café in Sewanee, Tennessee. It's a classic French preparation, combining the freshness of locally caught rainbow trout, the decadence of butter-browned almonds, and the brightness of freshly squeezed lemon juice.

TROUT ALMONDINE

Serves 4

4 (4-ounce) skin-on, boneless rainbow trout fillets (from 2 fish)	½ cup sliced natural almonds
	2 teaspoons minced shallot
Kosher salt and freshly ground black pepper	1 teaspoon chopped fresh flat-leaf parsley
2 tablespoons canola oil	1 teaspoon chopped fresh thyme
5 tablespoons unsalted butter	1½ tablespoons fresh lemon juice

1. Pat the fish dry with a paper towel, then lightly sprinkle both sides with the salt and pepper.

2. Place two Lodge 8-inch cast iron skillets over high heat. Add 1 tablespoon of the oil and ½ tablespoon of the butter to each skillet. When the butter is melted, add 2 fillets, flesh side down, to each skillet, and cook over high heat for about 4 minutes. (Note: After 2 minutes, carefully slide a metal spatula under the fish to ensure it is not sticking.) Turn the fillets over (the fish should be nicely browned but not dark), and cook for another 2 to 3 minutes. Carefully remove the trout to warm serving plates. Remove one skillet from the heat.

3. Add the remaining 4 tablespoons butter to the other skillet, and melt over high heat. Add the almonds, and swirl the pan to coat them with the butter. Cook for a minute or so. Add the shallot, parsley, thyme, and salt and pepper (a nice pinch of each should do). Toss the almonds constantly over the heat until they become uniformly light brown. Turn off the heat, add the lemon juice, and toss. The mixture will sizzle and foam. Top each fillet with the almond mixture.

This recipe from chef, caterer, and food writer Tamie Cook combines fresh basil and lemon zest to make the cakes tangy and light. The watercress salad completes it for the perfect lunch or light dinner.

TROUT CAKES AND WATERCRESS SALAD WITH BASIL VINAIGRETTE

Serves 4

- 1 pound skinless U.S. farm-raised trout fillets, pin bones removed
- ¾ cup panko breadcrumbs
- ½ cup red bell pepper, cut into small pieces
- Grated zest of 1 lemon
- 2 tablespoons chopped fresh basil
- 1 garlic clove, minced
- 1 large egg, beaten
- 1 teaspoon fine sea salt
- 1 tablespoon olive oil
- 8 cups watercress, rinsed and spun dry
- Basil Vinaigrette (recipe follows)

1. Place the trout fillets in the freezer until they begin to firm up but are not frozen, about 30 minutes.
2. While the fillets chill, combine the panko, bell pepper, lemon zest, basil, garlic, egg, and salt in a medium bowl.
3. Coarsely chop the chilled trout, and add to the bowl. Stir to combine. Divide the mixture into 4 equal portions, and shape into cakes about ½ inch thick.
4. Heat the oil in a Lodge 12-inch cast iron skillet over medium heat until it shimmers. Add the trout cakes to the pan, and cook until golden brown, about 4 minutes per side. Remove to a paper towel-lined plate to stand for 5 minutes.
5. To serve, toss the watercress with ¼ cup of the vinaigrette, and serve with the trout cakes, drizzled with additional vinaigrette, if desired.

BASIL VINAIGRETTE

Makes ½ cup

- 1 cup packed fresh basil leaves
- 1 garlic clove, peeled
- Generous pinch of fine sea salt
- Freshly ground black pepper to taste
- ¼ cup olive oil, plus more if needed
- 2 tablespoons Champagne vinegar

Place all the ingredients in a small food processor, and process until pureed. Add 1 to 2 tablespoons more oil, if desired, after tasting. Refrigerate in an airtight container for up to 3 days. Remove from the refrigerator 20 to 30 minutes prior to using so the olive oil is not solidified.

Says Jerry Clepper, a fan of Lodge, "A big catch in the Tennessee River calls for a Clepper family gathering. The fried fish never makes it to the table because it's gobbled up by the cook and the samplers as soon as it gets done." You can also fry French fries and hush puppies in the oil after all the fish has been cooked. Serve it all up with coleslaw, tartar sauce, and ketchup. If you like, you can substitute 6 cups of Zatarain's Fish Fri for the flour and cornmeal.

DEEP-FRIED CATFISH

Serves 10 to 12

1 gallon canola oil	Salt and freshly ground black pepper
3 cups all-purpose flour	
3 cups cornmeal	1 small jar yellow mustard
5 pounds catfish fillets, all cut to about the same size	Lemon wedges for garnish

1. Mount a Lodge 17-inch cast iron skillet on a propane burner in an outdoor cooking area. Fill the skillet two-thirds full with the oil. Heat the oil to 360°F. (Have a guest keep a watchful eye on it; it's best to use a deep-fry thermometer to track the temperature.)

2. Combine the flour and cornmeal in a clean paper grocery bag. Arrange the fish fillets in a single layer on wax paper-lined baking sheets. Season both sides of the fish with the salt and pepper to taste. Brush each piece on both sides with about ⅛ teaspoon of the mustard. Drop each fillet into the flour mixture, and shake the bag to coat well.

3. Before you start frying, have another clean paper bag lined with several paper towels and a slotted spoon ready at the cooker.

4. Place the fillets, one at a time, into the hot oil. Be careful not to overcrowd the pan or the temperature of the oil will drop and you won't get crispy fish. Using the slotted spoon, remove the fish soon after they float but not until they have turned light brown. Place the cooked fillets inside the clean grocery bag to drain and keep warm. Garnish with the lemon wedges.

Elizabeth Heiskell, lead culinary instructor at the Viking Cooking School in Greenwood, Mississippi, and author of the cookbook *What Can I Bring?*, contributed this recipe on behalf of her good friend Nan. "Only she could turn leftover fried catfish into pure genius," says Elizabeth.

NANNIE'S CATFISH CAKES

Serves 4; makes 8 (2½-inch) cakes

- 1 sleeve premium saltine crackers
- 2 tablespoons butter
- ¼ cup finely diced onion
- ¼ cup finely diced yellow bell pepper
- ¼ cup chopped green onions
- 8 fried catfish fillets
- 4 large eggs, lightly beaten
- 4 teaspoons Tabasco sauce
- 4 teaspoons Worcestershire sauce

Salt and freshly ground black pepper

- ¼ cup olive oil

Come Back Sauce (recipe at right)

1. Place the crackers in a food processor, and grind to crumbs; pour the crumbs into a shallow bowl.

2. Melt the butter in a medium Lodge cast iron skillet over medium heat. Add the onion, bell pepper, and green onions; cook, stirring often, until tender.

3. Place the catfish fillets in a medium bowl, and use your fingers or the back of a fork to mash them into bits. Add the beaten eggs, Tabasco, and Worcestershire; season with the salt and pepper to taste. Add the onion mixture, and stir well. Pat the catfish mixture into 8 cakes about 2½ inches wide and 1½ inches thick. Gently dredge the cakes in the cracker crumbs, coating well on both sides.

4. Heat a Lodge 12-inch cast iron skillet over medium-high heat, and add the oil. Gently place the catfish cakes in the hot skillet, and cook, in batches, until golden brown on both sides. Drain on a paper bag, and serve with Come Back Sauce.

This sauce originated at the Mayflower Cafe in Jackson, Mississippi, where it was the house salad dressing. It got its name because diners kept "coming back" for it. (Except, so the story goes in her family, Elizabeth Heiskell's cousin, who, after enjoying his salad with Come Back Sauce and one too many glasses of wine, was very politely asked *not* to come back.) Come Back Sauce pairs well with any kind of fried food (try fried green tomatoes) and also makes a tasty dip for cold boiled shrimp.

COME BACK SAUCE

Makes about 1¼ cups

- 1 tablespoon grated onion (using the large holes of a box grater)
- 1 cup mayonnaise
- 3 tablespoons fresh lemon juice
- 1 tablespoon vegetable oil
- 1 tablespoon prepared chili sauce
- 1 tablespoon Worcestershire sauce
- 1 teaspoon dry mustard
- 1 teaspoon salt
- 1 teaspoon freshly ground black pepper

Combine all the ingredients in a medium bowl, and stir well. If the sauce is too thick to drizzle, add 1 tablespoon water to thin. Refrigerate in an airtight container for up to 2 weeks.

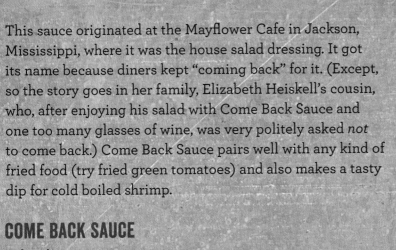

"Catfish is one of the few things openly accepted by ranchers and cattlemen as an alternative to beef," states Tom Perini, owner of Perini Ranch Steakhouse in Buffalo Gap, Texas. "Catfish can be found in most every river, lake, and pond in Texas, and we all grew up fishing for them." Now you can find farm-raised catfish in most every supermarket across the country, but for the best quality, buy fish raised in the U.S.

TEXAS FRIED CATFISH

Serves 6

6 (5- to 7-ounce) U.S. farm-raised catfish fillets

EGG DIP
¾ cup whole milk
1 large egg, beaten
2 teaspoons seasoning salt
½ teaspoon ground white pepper

SEASONED CORNMEAL
2 cups yellow cornmeal
¼ cup all-purpose flour
1 teaspoon salt
1 teaspoon cayenne pepper
½ teaspoon freshly ground black pepper
¼ teaspoon onion powder
¼ teaspoon garlic powder
Vegetable oil

1. Slice each fillet in half lengthwise. Prepare the Egg Dip and the Seasoned Cornmeal: In a shallow bowl, combine the egg dip ingredients, and mix well. On a large plate, combine the ingredients for the seasoned cornmeal.
2. Heat enough oil over medium-high heat to 350°F so that the fish fillets will be submerged in a Lodge 7-quart cast iron Dutch oven.
3. While the oil heats, dip the catfish fillets, one at a time, in the egg dip, coating each piece fully and letting any excess drip off. Dredge each piece in the seasoned cornmeal, coating it completely. Shake off any excess.
4. When the oil is hot, carefully slip the fillets into the oil without crowding them (you may have to fry them in batches). Fry until the fillets float to the top of the oil, about 6 minutes. When the fish is ready, the meat will be flaky. Transfer them to a wire rack to drain.

"This recipe is the height of simplicity," says Matt Moore. When that's the case, it means the ingredients used need to be of top quality. Matt buys his bacon from Benton's Smoky Mountain Country Hams in Madisonville, Tennessee, where it's smoked over an old-fashioned hickory wood-stoked stove. If you can find a Meyer lemon, please use it—a cross between a lemon and mandarin orange, it supplies great lemon flavor without the tart bite.

PAN-SEARED SEA SCALLOPS
Serves 2

¼ pound hickory-smoked bacon, finely diced

1 tablespoon unsalted butter

1 tablespoon extra-virgin olive oil

1 pound sea scallops, patted dry

½ lemon, preferably Meyer

Finely chopped fresh flat-leaf parsley for garnish

1. Heat a Lodge 12-inch cast iron skillet over medium heat for 1 minute. Add the bacon, and cook, stirring a few times, until it is crisp and the fat has rendered. Using a slotted spoon, transfer the bacon to a paper towel-lined plate to drain.

2. Add the butter and oil to the bacon drippings, and heat over medium-high heat until the butter melts. Add the scallops, and cook for 60 seconds on one side—do not touch. Flip the scallops, squeeze the lemon juice over them, and cook for another 60 to 90 seconds, until the scallops are just firm to the touch.

3. Remove the skillet from the heat, plate, and pour the pan drippings over the tops of the scallops. Sprinkle with the bacon, garnish with the parsley, and serve.

A COOKING SECRET FROM MATT

Choose dry-packed sea scallops (no water solution injected) for the best flavor and a good sear.

SEASONED WITH LOVE

Matt Moore

Author of Have Her Over for Dinner, A Southern Gentleman's Kitchen, *and* The South's Best Butts, *Nashville, Tennessee*

Speaking of pride, ma'ams and sirs, and what I was raised to do or not do, I'll say that my father, a Southern gentleman himself, taught me, with an ear-to-ear grin, to open doors for women right alongside the ways and means of sipping a dark drink. Momma, on the other hand, taught me how to charm and cook. But it was her mother, my grandmother Sitty, as she was known, who schooled me on the ins and outs of cooking with Lodge cast iron. On Sundays, my grandfather Giddy, who by trade was a butcher, would bring home cuts of meat carefully trimmed and preserved by his skilled hands. Sitty would cook and stew all morning long—stopping only to put on her face and attend Sunday services. When we returned to their Valdosta, Georgia, home afterward, family, friends, preacher men, and strangers would all gather to enjoy her Southern splendor at the family table.

The spread, just like the conversation, seemed to stretch for miles. Skillet fried chicken, collards, mac 'n' cheese, cornbread, fried okra, biscuits—the Southern staples—were all served right alongside the Middle Eastern favorites from my grandparents' youth: hummus, tabbouleh, kibbeh, and stuffed grape leaves. Together, we lived, ate, cooked, and learned.

Though my grandparents have since passed, those memories and lessons of family and food continue to impact my own life. Their passing did not bequeath me a wealth of monetary goods; rather it was my grandmother's Lodge cast iron skillets that made their way into my hands to cherish forever.

Nowadays, I do most of the work in the kitchen, entertaining family, friends, and strangers just as those who came before me did. Yet I know that I am never alone. As ingredients sizzle and pop in my inherited cast iron pans, I know that my guests will soon savor and enjoy another great meal. For me, I find comfort in knowing that my recipes always taste a bit better coming out of my grandmother's skillets, as they are all seasoned with the very best ingredient in any kitchen—love.

Jambalaya is traditionally cooked on the stove-top, but in this oven version from Atlanta-based chef and cookbook author Virginia Willis, the rice is perfect every time.

VIRGINIA WILLIS' SEAFOOD AND CHICKEN JAMBALAYA

Serves 4 to 6

- 1 tablespoon canola oil
- 4 skinless, bone-in chicken thighs (about 1½ pounds)
- Coarse kosher salt and freshly ground black pepper
- 6 ounces andouille sausage, sliced
- 1 tablespoon Cajun or Creole seasoning
- 1 medium sweet onion, chopped
- 1 celery rib, chopped
- ½ red bell pepper, seeded and chopped
- 1 garlic clove, very finely chopped
- 1½ cups uncooked long-grain rice
- 1 (8-ounce) can tomato sauce
- 2 cups homemade chicken stock, reduced-fat/low-sodium chicken broth, or water
- 1 bay leaf, preferably fresh
- 1 pound large (21/25 count) shrimp, peeled and deveined

1. Preheat the oven to 350°F.

2. Heat the oil in a Lodge 12-inch cast iron skillet over medium-high heat until shimmering. Season the chicken with the salt and pepper on both sides, and add to the hot oil. Cook until browned on both sides, 3 to 5 minutes total. Remove to a plate.

3. Pour off any rendered fat in the skillet, and discard. Add the andouille, and cook, stirring occasionally, until the meat starts to brown and render fat, about 3 minutes. Add the Cajun seasoning, and stir to combine. Add the onion, celery, and bell pepper; cook, stirring occasionally, until the vegetables start to color, 5 to 7 minutes. Add the garlic, and cook until fragrant, 45 to 60 seconds. Add the rice, and stir to coat. Stir in the tomato sauce and stock, and bring to a boil. Return the seared chicken thighs to the skillet, and nestle them, without crowding, into the rice. Tuck the bay leaf into the rice. Transfer to the oven, and bake, uncovered, for 30 minutes.

4. Add the shrimp, and stir to combine. Continue to bake, uncovered, until the rice is tender, the shrimp are opaque, and the juices of the chicken run clear when pierced with the tip of a knife, signifying the chicken is done, about 10 minutes. Remove the skillet from the oven to a wire rack to cool slightly. Add the salt and pepper to taste. Remove the bay leaf, and serve immediately.

A COOKING SECRET FROM VIRGINIA

Don't cover the jambalaya while it's cooking in the oven. Keeping the pan uncovered allows the excess liquid from the broth and tomatoes to evaporate and the rice to cook evenly.

This version of the classic rice dish (which is a Southern coastal interpretation of paella) is from Steven Satterfield, executive chef/co-owner of Miller Union in Atlanta. A few things are crucial to the final flavor of the dish. The first is using Carolina Gold rice, an heirloom variety of long-grain rice that is hand-harvested by its producer Anson Mills (buy it online at ansonmills.com). Secondly, sautéing the rice in fat for a good 5 minutes helps to infuse flavor into the individual grains. Lastly, no peeking while the rice is cooking—the covered cast iron pot is key to the development of the crust on the bottom. Steven likes to serve this with a green salad and roasted okra.

SAVANNAH RED RICE

Serves 6

- 4 tablespoons bacon drippings
- 5 tablespoons butter
- 1 small yellow onion, diced
- 1 cup diced celery (inner leaves included)
- 2 garlic cloves, minced
- 2 tablespoons plus 1 teaspoon kosher salt or more to taste
- 2 cups canned organic whole plum tomatoes, undrained, chopped
- 2 cups chicken stock
- 2 tablespoons pepper vinegar or cider vinegar (if you use cider vinegar, add a pinch of red pepper flakes)
- 1¼ teaspoons freshly ground black pepper
- ¾ teaspoon dried thyme
- 2 bay leaves
- 2 dried chiles de arbol, chopped, or a pinch of red pepper flakes
- 2 cups long-grain rice (such as Carolina Gold)
- ½ pound andouille or chorizo sausage, grilled and sliced ½ inch thick
- 1 pound shrimp, peeled, deveined, and cut into bite-size pieces

1. Heat 2 tablespoons of the bacon drippings and 2 tablespoons of the butter in a medium saucepan over medium heat until melted. Add the onion, celery, garlic, and 1 tablespoon of the salt; cook, stirring often, until the onion and garlic are tender. Add the tomatoes, stock, vinegar, 1 tablespoon of the salt, 1 teaspoon of the black pepper, the thyme, bay leaves, and chiles; simmer 15 to 20 minutes, tasting for seasoning.

2. Heat the remaining 2 tablespoons bacon drippings and 2 tablespoons of the butter in a large Lodge cast iron skillet over medium heat until foamy. Add the rice, and cook, stirring frequently, until it is opaque, about 5 minutes. This step is very important to the

final flavor of the dish, so don't skimp on the time—but also don't let the rice burn.

3. Add 4 cups of the tomato mixture to the rice; stir to combine, and cover. Set a timer, and cook the rice for 25 minutes over very low heat. DO NOT LIFT THE LID. After 25 minutes, turn off the heat and let the rice stand for 5 more minutes. AGAIN, DO NOT LIFT THE LID. While the rice cooks, add the sausage to the remaining tomato mixture in the pan; cover and keep warm over very low heat.

4. While the rice is standing, melt the remaining 1 tablespoon butter in a medium sauté pan over medium-high heat until foamy. Add the shrimp, and cook, stirring just until cooked through; add the remaining 1 teaspoon salt and ¼ teaspoon black pepper. Add the shrimp to the sausage and tomato mixture, and stir well.

5. Pour the shrimp and sausage mixture over the rice. Remove and discard the bay leaves. Gently fluff the rice (you don't want to break the grains) to combine. Serve immediately.

LEMONGRASS SHRIMP

Serves 2 to 4

- ¼ cup canola oil
- 2 lemongrass stalks (see Kitchen Note), bruised and cut into 2-inch lengths
- 1 pound large (26/30 count) shrimp, peeled, deveined, and patted dry
- 3 tablespoons Thai fish sauce
- 3 tablespoons fresh lime juice
- 1½ tablespoons sugar

- 1 shallot, thinly sliced
- 2 tablespoons thinly sliced lemongrass (from skinny section at top of stalk)
- 1 or 2 Thai chiles, finely chopped
- ¼ cup chopped fresh cilantro
- ¼ cup fresh mint leaves
- 2 cups cooked jasmine rice, cooked according to package directions

Cooking school teacher and cookbook author Naam Pruitt's hometown, Prachuabkirikhan, is located on the Gulf of Thailand, so she and seafood are no strangers to one another. And even though she now lives in St. Louis, Missouri, she still prepares seafood for her family every day.

1. Heat a Lodge 12-inch cast iron skillet over high heat. Add the oil, and wait until it is hot. Add the bruised lemongrass pieces, and cook until lightly browned, about 5 minutes, stirring occasionally. Add the shrimp, and cook until pink, turning them several times, 3 to 4 minutes. Turn off the heat. Transfer the shrimp to a large bowl. Discard the lemongrass pieces.

2. Add the fish sauce, lime juice, sugar, shallot, sliced lemongrass, chiles, cilantro, and mint to the shrimp, mixing well. Serve with the jasmine rice.

KITCHEN NOTE:

Fresh lemongrass is crucial for this recipe, its lemony essence infusing the shrimp as it cooks. When buying lemongrass, size matters; the thicker the stalks, the stronger the flavor. A good rule of thumb is to use thick stalks for cooking and skinnier ones in salads and other preparations where it will be used raw.

How Naam Slices Lemongrass

1. Trim off the very end of the stalk before using.

2. Use a meat mallet or heavy pestle to bruise the lemongrass, pounding the entire stalk. Doing this will release the essential oil for its distinctive aroma.

3. To slice lemongrass, you need to use the more tender part of the stalk at the top; the lower part of the stalk is much too fibrous to eat.

This stir-fry comes from Asian cooking expert and cookbook author Nancie McDermott. She based it on the Thai dish chicken with holy basil (*gai paht bai graprao*), substituting shrimp—which, though not typical, is delicious and gorgeous—adding more onion and less chile heat, and using sweet Thai basil. It's wonderful served over rice, orzo, or couscous, or offered up with a salad or garlicky sautéed greens and good crusty bread and butter.

SHRIMP with FRESH BASIL, THAI STYLE

Serves 3 to 4

2 tablespoons Asian fish sauce	1 tablespoon chopped garlic
2 tablespoons water	¼ cup finely chopped green onions
1 teaspoon soy sauce	
½ teaspoon sugar	2 tablespoons coarsely chopped fresh cilantro
2 tablespoons vegetable oil	
1 pound medium shrimp, peeled and deveined	1 tablespoon seeded and chopped jalapeño, serrano, or other green chile
1 cup thinly sliced onion (sliced into half moons and pulled apart into strips)	¾ cup loosely packed fresh Thai or other basil leaves

1. Stir together the fish sauce, water, soy sauce, and sugar in a small bowl, and set aside. Prep the remaining ingredients, so you can add them quickly when they are needed.

2. Place a Lodge 10- or 12-inch cast iron skillet over medium-high heat until it becomes very hot, about 30 seconds.

3. Add the oil, and turn to coat the pan evenly. Add the shrimp in a single layer, and leave them to cook on one side, undisturbed, until their edges turn bright pink. Toss well, and turn all the shrimp cooked side up so the other side can cook, undisturbed, for 15 seconds.

4. Add the onion and garlic, and toss well. Cook 1 minute, tossing occasionally, until the onion softens and becomes fragrant and shiny; continue tossing so it wilts and softens but doesn't brown.

5. Stir the fish sauce mixture to make sure the sugar is dissolved, and pour it around the edge of the pan. Toss well to season the shrimp with the sauce, then let cook, undisturbed, just until the shrimp are cooked through and the sauce is bubbling. (The sauce will not be thick; it will have the consistency of thin pan juices.)

6. Add the green onions, cilantro, and chile, and toss well. Tear any big basil leaves into 2 or 3 pieces each (you want to tear the basil at the very last minute, otherwise it will darken). Add all of the basil to the pan over the shrimp, and toss well. Cook 10 seconds, and pour onto a serving platter deep enough to hold a little sauce. Serve hot.

Often in Pensacola on assignment, and having a husband who works and resides there as well, Susan Benton, food writer and owner of 30AEATS.com, enjoys frequenting Joe Patti's Seafood. Susan says, "It is an experience! Like our own little version of Seattle's Pike Place Market, yet here on the Gulf Coast!" Pick up a container or two of fresh, succulent jumbo lump Gulf crab, and try your hand at making this decadent recipe using Lodge cast iron individual tabletop servers.

JUMBO LUMP GULF CRABMEAT AU GRATIN

Serves 4

½ cup (1 stick) unsalted butter

1 medium onion, finely chopped

1 celery rib, finely chopped

2 tablespoons chopped green onion (white part only)

1 teaspoon minced garlic

2 large egg yolks, slightly beaten

1 (12-ounce) can evaporated milk

½ cup all-purpose flour

1 teaspoon kosher salt

½ teaspoon cayenne pepper

½ teaspoon freshly ground black pepper

2 cups (8 ounces) finely grated Gruyère cheese

1 pound jumbo lump Gulf crabmeat, picked over for shells and cartilage

1 tablespoon minced fresh parsley

1. Preheat the oven to 350°F.

2. Melt the butter in a Lodge 10-inch cast iron skillet over medium-high heat. Add the onion, celery, green onions, and garlic, and cook, stirring, until the vegetables are wilted, 3 to 5 minutes.

3. While the vegetables cook, vigorously whisk the egg yolks and evaporated milk together in a small bowl until well blended; set aside.

4. Add the flour to the skillet, and blend well into the vegetables to create a white roux; don't let the flour brown. Using a wire whisk, add the milk mixture, stirring constantly to blend into the roux mixture. Stir in the salt, cayenne, and black pepper, and continue to stir for another 3 to 5 minutes. Remove from the heat, and fold in half the cheese; blend until it is totally melted and fully incorporated.

5. Gently divide the crabmeat among 4 Lodge 9-ounce cast iron mini servers; try not to break apart the lumps. Top evenly with the cheese sauce, then sprinkle with the remaining grated cheese. Cover and bake until bubbly, about 15 minutes. Increase the oven to broil, and broil until the cheese begins to brown, about 5 minutes. Remove from the oven, and sprinkle with the parsley before serving.

PENN COVE MUSSELS WITH CHORIZO, GARLIC TOASTS, AND AÏOLI

Serves 2 as a main course, 4 as a hearty appetizer

A mellow, smoky paprika aïoli complements both the spicy sausage and the sweet sea flavor of the mussels in this preparation from Seattle-based chef/restaurateur Tom Douglas. And the crunch of a slice of golden, crusty, toasted bread is mandatory alongside a bowl of mussels! Tom says to be sure to buy Spanish chorizo, which is different from Mexican chorizo. And if your cast iron skillet doesn't have a lid, use a baking sheet to cover it when steaming the mussels.

SMOKED PAPRIKA AÏOLI

- ½ cup mayonnaise
- 2 teaspoons fresh lemon juice
- 2 teaspoons smoked Spanish paprika
- ½ teaspoon grated lemon zest
- Kosher salt and freshly ground black pepper

MUSSELS

- 2 tablespoons olive oil
- ½ cup finely chopped onion
- ½ cup chopped Spanish chorizo (about 3 ounces)
- 2 cups canned crushed or chopped tomatoes, undrained
- ½ cup dry white wine
- Kosher salt and freshly ground black pepper
- 2 pounds mussels, rinsed, scrubbed, and beards removed (discard any mussels that won't close)

GARLIC TOASTS

- 2 or 3 garlic cloves, peeled
- 4 slices rustic bread, ½ to ¾ inch thick
- Olive oil as needed for brushing
- Kosher salt and freshly ground black pepper

GARNISH

- 4 lemon wedges (optional)

1. Prepare the Smoked Paprika Aïoli: In a small bowl, combine the mayonnaise, lemon juice, paprika, and lemon zest. Season with the salt and pepper to taste. Cover the aïoli, and refrigerate until ready to use and up to one day.

2. Prepare the Mussels: Put a Lodge 12-inch cast iron skillet over medium-high heat, and add the oil. When the oil is hot, add the onion, and cook, stirring, until softened, about 3 minutes. Add the chorizo, and sauté for a minute or two. Add the tomatoes and wine, and bring to a simmer; continue to simmer (reducing the heat as needed) until the sauce thickens, 10 to 15 minutes. Season to taste with the salt and pepper. Add the mussels to the skillet, increase the heat to medium-high or high, cover the pan, and cook until the mussels open, about 5 minutes. (Discard any mussels that won't open.)

3. While the mussels cook, prepare the Garlic Toasts: Preheat the broiler. Smash the garlic cloves with the back of a knife. Rub the slices of bread on one side with the smashed garlic. Brush both sides of the bread with the oil, and season with the salt and pepper. Toast the bread slices under the broiler, turning once, until golden and toasted, a minute or two per side.

4. Divide the mussels between 2 shallow soup bowls. Place a dollop of aïoli on each toast, and place a toast on the rim of each soup bowl. Serve immediately, garnished with lemon wedges, if desired.

This simple recipe comes from the mother-daughter team of cookbook authors and cast iron aficionados Sharon Kramis and Julie Kramis Hearne. Mussels should be cooked until their shells open up, and they are plump and juicy; if they don't open, don't eat them. Serve this delicious dish with a crusty loaf of your favorite bread to sop up all the tasty juices!

IRON SKILLET ROASTED MUSSELS

Serves 6

½ cup white wine
¼ cup (½ stick) unsalted butter
1 leek (white part only), rinsed well and chopped
¼ teaspoon red pepper flakes
2 pounds mussels, scrubbed and debearded (discard any mussels that don't close)

3 tablespoons chopped fresh parsley
Salt and freshly ground black pepper

1. Combine the wine, butter, leek, and red pepper in a Lodge 10- to 12-inch cast iron skillet or Lodge 5-quart cast iron Dutch oven, and bring to a boil over medium-high heat.

2. Reduce the heat to medium; add the mussels, and cover. Cook until the shells open and the mussels are plump, about 8 minutes. (Discard any mussels that don't open.)

3. Sprinkle the parsley over the top, and season with the salt and pepper to taste. Serve right from the skillet or Dutch oven with sliced bread.

⤜ SIDES ⤛

Don't reserve Lodge cast iron only for main
dish roasts and center-stage stews. Use it to
make these spectacular side dishes as well.
A sundry of vegetables becomes Farmers'
Market Ratatouille, puréed onions and
potatoes transform into Potato "Lodgekes,"
and other humble ingredients come to life
when cooked in cast iron.

FARMERS' MARKET RATATOUILLE

Serves 6

This recipe comes from Donita Anderson, executive director of North Union Farmers' Market in Cleveland, Ohio. Not surprisingly, she sources almost all the ingredients for this dish from the market: olive oil from Olive Tap, eggplant from Walnut Drive Gardens, onions from Gingerich Farm, fresh garlic from Maximum Garlic Farm, tomatoes from Heritage Lane Farm and Rainbow Farm, red peppers from Weaver's Truck Patch, summer squash from Crooked Creek, zucchini from Don Anna, and fresh herbs from Rainbow Farm and Snake Hill Farm.

1 large round eggplant, peeled and cut into ½-inch pieces
Sea salt
2 tablespoons extra-virgin olive oil, plus more as needed
1 large white onion, cut into ¼-inch pieces
Pinch of red pepper flakes
4 garlic cloves, smashed and finely chopped
3 large tomatoes, cut into ½-inch pieces
4 plum tomatoes, cut into ½-inch pieces
½ cup water
2 tablespoons good-quality red wine
1 teaspoon good-quality balsamic vinegar
1 teaspoon fresh thyme leaves
½ teaspoon crushed dried rosemary
2 medium red bell peppers, seeded and cut into ½-inch pieces
2 medium summer squash, cut into ½-inch pieces
2 medium zucchini, cut into ½-inch pieces
6 to 8 fresh basil leaves, thinly sliced
Freshly ground black pepper
¾ cup grated Gruyère cheese
French bread or naan (optional)

1. Place the eggplant pieces on paper towels, and lightly salt. Let stand for 30 minutes to sweat. Mop up the moisture on the eggplant with more paper towels.
2. Heat a Lodge 12-inch cast iron skillet over medium-high heat. Add the oil, and swirl to coat the bottom of the pan. Add the eggplant, and cook, stirring a few times, until browned; remove from the pan, and set aside.
3. Add a little more oil, the onion, red pepper, and salt to taste, and cook over medium heat, stirring a few times, until the onion is softened and very aromatic, 7 to 8 minutes; don't allow the onion to color. Add the garlic, and cook, stirring, for 2 to 3 minutes. Add the tomatoes, water, wine, vinegar, thyme, and rosemary, and season with the salt to taste. Simmer, uncovered, until the tomatoes become very pulpy and have broken apart, 15 to 20 minutes.
4. Add the bell peppers, and cook for 5 minutes. Add the summer squash and zucchini, return the eggplant to the pan, season with the salt, and cook over low heat, uncovered, until the squash and eggplant are softened, 15 to 20 minutes.
5. Stir in the sliced basil, add the salt and pepper to taste, then simmer, covered, for 15 minutes.
6. Sprinkle the Gruyère over the ratatouille while it's still warm in the pan. Serve warm or at room temperature over lightly toasted French bread or naan, if desired. Leftovers can be wrapped well and frozen.

Author and *Garden & Gun* contributing editor Julia Reed says, "In summer, I am spoiled by the fact that farmers' markets both in New Orleans, where I live, and near Seaside, Florida, where I go as often as I can, offer up zip-top bags of already cleaned and sliced okra, as well as shucked ears of corn. Two of my favorite dishes are okra and tomatoes and 'fried' corn, so one year I decided to combine the two." For a main course, Julia suggests adding some peeled fresh Gulf shrimp during the last few minutes (see Kitchen Note).

JULIA'S SUCCOTASH

Serves 6 to 8

- 6 bacon slices
- 1 medium yellow (or Vidalia) onion, minced
- 1 jalapeño chile, seeded and minced
- 3 cups sliced okra
- 4 ripe tomatoes, diced
- 4 garlic cloves, minced
- 1 teaspoon salt
- ½ teaspoon freshly ground black pepper
- 2 teaspoons chopped fresh thyme
- 6 ears fresh corn, husks removed
- Dash of cayenne pepper (optional)
- 8 fresh basil leaves, torn into pieces

1. Cook the bacon in a large Lodge cast iron skillet over medium-high heat until crisp. Remove the bacon to paper towels to drain, reserving the drippings in the pan.
2. Add the onion and jalapeño to the drippings in the skillet, and cook, stirring occasionally, over low or medium-low heat until the vegetables begin to soften, 4 to 5 minutes. Increase the heat to medium, add the okra, and cook for 5 minutes, stirring frequently. Add the tomatoes, garlic, salt, black pepper, and thyme. Reduce the heat to medium-low. Cook for another 3 to 4 minutes. Cut the kernels off the cobs. Discard the cobs. Add the corn, and simmer, partially covered, until it's tender, about 10 minutes, stirring occasionally.
3. Check and adjust the seasonings, and add a dash of the cayenne, if desired, and the basil. Crumble the reserved bacon, sprinkle it on top, and serve.

KITCHEN NOTE:

If you add shrimp, you may need to add a bit of liquid. Shrimp stock, chicken stock, or water will work fine.

For Mark Kelly, public relations and advertising manager for Lodge Manufacturing, one of the greatest pleasures of living in southeast Tennessee is enjoying the abundance of fresh produce it has to offer. He frequents the Chattanooga Market, which is open each Sunday in the spring, summer, and fall, and provides a wide selection of fresh-off-the-farm produce. One of Mark's favorite veggies to grill on his Lodge Sportsman's Grill is okra.

GRILLED OKRA

Serves 3

1 pound large fresh okra pods
1½ tablespoons kosher salt
½ teaspoon freshly ground
  black pepper
½ teaspoon garlic salt
2 tablespoons olive oil

1. Build a fire in a Lodge Sportsman's Grill, and allow the coals to burn low.
2. Meanwhile, rinse the okra under cold running water, and pat dry. (KEEP THE TIPS AND BOTTOMS.)
3. In a large bowl, stir together the salt, pepper, garlic salt, and oil. Add the okra, and toss until the pods are completely coated.
4. Place the okra on the grill using tongs, and turn after about 3 minutes, allowing the okra to become nicely browned. Remove from the grill, and serve.

CRAZY FOR CAST IRON

Mark Kelly

*Public relations and advertising manager of Lodge Manufacturing,
South Pittsburg, Tennessee*

OK, I confess. I wasn't much of a cook until the spring of 2005. That's when this former sports writer began meeting chefs, food stylists, cookbook authors, and other foodies while promoting Lodge Cast Iron Cookware. The more I became entrenched in the food world, the more I realized, "I can do this."

Strangely enough, my stove-top efforts with skillets, grill pans, and Dutch ovens weren't complete disasters (at least no one said they were calories of mass destruction).

Where I really found my niche was with the Lodge Sportsman's Grill, a highly revered all cast iron hibachi. Designed with a pull-down drawer to assist in the adding of more coals and a sliding door for airflow, it's easier to use than a smart phone.

But the truly utilitarian feature I most admire are the thin grill grates, which allow for the preparation of veggies, shrimp, fish, etc., without skewers and without worrying about food falling into the fire. The grill is equally proficient in preparing barbecued chicken or grilling steaks.

In my travels with Lodge, I've realized that food culture is in a constant state of change. A skillet may have its roots in cooking fried chicken, but the grandchildren of its original owner may be preparing stir-fries or fajitas in the same pan. Our Sportsman's Grill has a similar story. My recipes have a noticeable nod to the Deep South. Traveling around the country, though, I've seen folks tailgating at Southeastern Conference football games using their grill to prepare wings, burgers, and hot dogs. Many times their recipes feature Cajun or other regional spices. In the Midwest, you'll find bratwurst, venison, and perch fillets. In Texas and the Southwest, people will fire up their Sportsman's Grill with mesquite briquettes to cook beef briskets and a small skillet of peppers and onions. On the West Coast, the grill cooks everything from bluefin tuna to salmon, as well as tomatoes, onions, and other seasonal vegetables at home, at campsites, or when tailgating.

In the recipe collection of Lynda King Kellermann, wife of company founder Joseph Lodge's grandson Charles Richard "Dick" Kellermann, Jr., there is a recipe for Creole Cabbage with the notation "Mrs. D. F. Hobbs, Fayetteville, Tenn." Lynda boarded with Mrs. Hobbs and her family when she taught home economics. Mrs. Hobbs and her brother, Robert Buchanan, owned *The Lincoln County News*. In the 1940 U.S. Census, Mrs. Hobbs' occupation is listed as the social editor of a rural newspaper.

CREOLE CABBAGE

Serves 6

- 2 tablespoons vegetable oil or bacon drippings
- 1 medium head cabbage, cored and shredded
- 1 medium green bell pepper, seeded and chopped
- 1 medium onion, chopped
- 1 (15-ounce) can diced tomatoes, undrained, or 3 cups diced fresh tomatoes
- Salt
- Cayenne pepper

Heat the oil in a Lodge 12-inch cast iron skillet over medium heat. Add the cabbage, bell pepper, and onion, and stir to combine. Pour over the tomatoes, and season with the salt and cayenne to taste. Simmer until the cabbage, onion, and pepper are tender, 20 to 30 minutes.

This was a springtime favorite of the late Marion and Bertha Gonce, who farmed the Joseph Lodge farm in South Pittsburg, Tennessee, starting in 1934. Bertha believed the salad is best when the lettuce, radishes, and onions are grown in your own garden and picked just before preparing.

WILTED LETTUCE SALAD

Serves 6

SALAD
- 1 head leaf lettuce (or spinach), torn
- 6 radishes, thinly sliced
- 4 to 6 green onions, thinly sliced
- 4 hard-cooked eggs, sliced

DRESSING
- 5 bacon slices
- 2 tablespoons red wine vinegar
- 1 tablespoon fresh lemon juice
- 1 teaspoon sugar
- ½ teaspoon freshly ground black pepper

1. Prepare the Salad: Toss together the lettuce, radishes, and green onions in a large bowl.

2. Prepare the Dressing: Cook the bacon in a Lodge 10-inch cast iron skillet over medium-high heat until crisp. Remove to paper towels to drain, reserving the drippings in the skillet, and crumble the bacon. Add the vinegar, lemon juice, sugar, and pepper to the drippings, and stir well. Immediately pour the dressing over the salad, and toss gently. Top with the sliced eggs, and sprinkle with the crumbled bacon. Serve immediately.

"There is no better dish than this one to show you the importance of cookware," declares Kelly English, chef-owner of Restaurant Iris and The Second Line in Memphis. "Go ahead. I dare you to try to cook this on anything but Lodge cast iron. This is the salad that my entire menu was built around."

"SALAD" OF BRUSSELS SPROUTS, BACON, AND SHERRY

Serves 4

- 2 pounds Brussels sprouts (Kelly gets his from Woodson Ridge Farms in Oxford, Mississippi)
- ½ cup olive oil
- 2 tablespoons sherry vinegar
- ¼ pound sliced bacon (Kelly likes to use Benton's hickory-smoked country bacon from Madisonville, Tennessee), cut across into strips

- 2 shallots, minced
- 4 garlic cloves, minced
- 2 tablespoons fresh thyme leaves
- Kosher salt and freshly ground black pepper

1. Bring a large pot of very salty (salty like the ocean) water to a boil.
2. Trim the stems of the Brussels sprouts, then cut them in half through the stem. Blanch the sprouts in the boiling water until tender but not mushy, about 2 minutes. Drain, then shock the sprouts in ice water to stop the cooking, and drain again.
3. In a small bowl, make a vinaigrette by whisking the oil and vinegar together until thickened (emulsified).
4. In a Lodge 15-inch cast iron skillet over medium heat, cook the bacon; when it begins to crisp and the fat is released, add the sprouts. Cook, stirring a few times, until the sprouts start to take on good color, about 1 minute. Add the shallots, garlic, and thyme, toss to combine, and cook, stirring, until the shallots become translucent.
5. Pour the vinaigrette over the salad (still in the skillet) to coat, and season with the salt and pepper to taste.

This recipe from Scott Jones, food and wine expert and former executive food editor of *Southern Living*, is an update to his grandmother's recipe (and a childhood favorite). "My Mema used a smoked hock in her greens, along with a generous shake of hot sauce and pinch of sugar. I get my subtle sweet-tart pop from balsamic vinegar and the heat from red pepper flakes." Scott made the recipe a tad healthier by using bacon and fat-free chicken broth, which also creates a cleaner-tasting pot likker. Scott has been known to ladle the greens and pot likker over a bowl of creamy stone-ground grits.

SCOTT'S COLLARDS

Serves 8

- 4 bacon slices
- 1 large carrot, chopped
- 1 large onion, chopped
- 2 garlic cloves, minced
- 2 to 3 tablespoons balsamic vinegar
- 4 (1-pound) packages fresh collard greens, washed, trimmed, and chopped
- 1½ cups low-sodium fat-free chicken broth
- ½ teaspoon red pepper flakes
- ½ teaspoon salt
- ¼ teaspoon freshly ground black pepper

1. Cook the bacon in a Lodge cast iron Dutch oven over medium-high heat until crisp. Remove the bacon to paper towels to drain, reserving 2 tablespoons of the drippings in the pot. Crumble the bacon.

2. Cook the carrot in the hot bacon drippings over medium-high heat, stirring occasionally, for 5 minutes. Add the onion, and cook, stirring occasionally, until the carrot and onion begin to caramelize, about 5 minutes. Add the garlic; cook 30 seconds, stirring constantly. Add the vinegar, and cook 30 seconds. Add the collards, crumbled bacon, broth, red pepper, salt, and black pepper. Bring to a boil; cover, reduce the heat to a simmer, and cook until the collards are tender, about 1 hour.

This recipe is from Beth Duggar, president of the National Cornbread Festival, which is held each year in Lodge's hometown of South Pittsburg, Tennessee. Beth offers this tip for freezing okra from the garden: "Take it straight from the garden, and put it directly into freezer bags. When ready to use, thaw and wash. This way the okra holds its pleasing 'slime,' which is what makes it great!"

SOUTHERN FRIED OKRA

Serves 4 to 6 people who love okra

- 2 quarts fresh okra
- 1 to 2 large eggs, lightly beaten
- About 1 cup cornmeal
- 1 teaspoon salt or to taste
- ¼ teaspoon freshly ground black pepper or to taste
- ½ teaspoon onion powder or garlic powder (optional)
- ½ to ¾ cup bacon drippings or vegetable oil (enough to fill the skillet ¼ inch deep)

1. Wash the okra with lots of water, and let dry. Remove the ends, and slice into ¼- to ½-inch-thick rounds; place in a large bowl. (If the okra is tough, throw it out.) Pour the beaten egg(s) over the okra, and stir gently until the rounds are coated. Add the cornmeal, salt, pepper, and, if desired, onion or garlic powder, stirring gently to coat.

2. Heat the bacon drippings in a Lodge 12-inch cast iron skillet over medium-high heat until hot. To test, add a slice of okra to the skillet to see if it really sizzles. Pour half the okra into the skillet, and cook until golden brown all over, turning it with a metal spatula. (Some people like it almost burned.) You may need to add more bacon drippings.

3. Remove the okra from the skillet, and repeat with the remaining okra, adding more drippings if needed.

This recipe grew out of a small backyard-farming project on the grounds at *Sunset* magazine and was contributed by Margo True, food editor at *Sunset*. For a series of seasonal dinners, Margo and her team cooked only what they could raise or grow. Later the team wrote a book about their adventures, with recipes, called *The One-Block Feast*. Cipollini onions were one of Margo's favorite crops from the project—she loves their dense sweetness—and she still cooks them all the time.

ROASTED CIPOLLINI ONIONS WITH CHILE-ROSEMARY BUTTER

Serves 4

- 1 pound cipollini onions
- 1 tablespoon olive oil
- 2 teaspoons chopped fresh rosemary
- Pinch or two of red pepper flakes
- Kosher salt
- 2 tablespoons butter

1. Preheat the oven to 400°F. Meanwhile, peel the onions.

2. Pour the oil into a Lodge 10-inch cast iron skillet. Add the onions, sprinkle with the rosemary and red pepper, and season with the salt to taste. Turn them over in the oil until thoroughly coated. Roast the onions until they're tender, about 30 minutes, turning them over every 10 minutes so they roast evenly.

3. Set the skillet on the stove-top over medium heat, and add the butter. Cook, stirring every now and then, just until the butter starts to brown, 1 to 2 minutes. Serve with a little of the butter spooned over the top.

This is a basic fritter recipe you can use with your favorite veggies like sweet corn, mushrooms, or, in this case, zucchini, because, says Felicia Willett, chef-owner of Felicia Suzanne's in downtown Memphis, "Let's face it, zucchini has a long season in the South!" You can make them small for cocktail parties and add a dollop of tomato jam (Felicia sells her own, sold under the brand Flo's). For dinner, make them a little larger, add a grilled piece of meat or fish, and top with fresh salsa.

ZUCCHINI FRITTERS

Makes 12 to 14 fritters

- 1 pound zucchini (8 to 10 small or 2 large), ends trimmed
- 1 cup (4 ounces) grated Parmesan cheese
- ½ cup chopped green onions
- ½ cup all-purpose flour
- 1 tablespoon baking powder
- 1 large egg, beaten
- Juice and grated zest of 1 lemon
- Kosher salt and freshly ground black pepper
- Hot sauce
- ½ cup olive oil

1. Preheat the oven to 350°F.

2. Using the large holes of a box grater, grate the zucchini onto a clean kitchen towel. Carefully squeeze out the liquid, and discard it. In a large bowl, combine the zucchini, Parmesan, and green onions, and mix well. In a small bowl, combine the flour and baking powder, and mix well. Add to the zucchini mixture along with the egg and lemon juice and zest; mix well. Season with the salt, pepper, and hot sauce.

3. Heat ¼ cup of the oil in a Lodge 12-inch cast iron skillet over medium heat. Spoon a heaping tablespoonful of the batter into the hot oil for each fritter, slightly pressing the batter down to form the cake. Fry until golden and crispy, about 2 minutes per side.

4. As the fritters finish cooking, transfer them to a parchment paper-lined baking sheet, and place in the oven to keep warm. Continue frying until all of the batter is used; add more of the remaining ¼ cup oil to the skillet as needed.

This recipe comes from Linton Hopkins, chef/owner of Restaurant Eugene and Holeman & Finch Public House in Atlanta.

SUMMER SQUASH CASSEROLE

Serves 8

8 yellow squash
¼ cup (½ stick) unsalted butter
1½ cups sliced Vidalia onion
2 garlic cloves, chopped
½ cup chopped fresh flat-leaf parsley
Salt and freshly ground black pepper
½ cup 1-inch pieces white bread slices with crusts removed

Ice water
2 large eggs, lightly beaten
1 sleeve saltine crackers, crushed into crumbs
2 tablespoons unsalted butter, cut into small pieces

1. Preheat the oven to 350°F. Butter 8 individual Lodge cast iron round mini servers.

2. Peel, then cut the squash crosswise into ⅛-inch-thick rounds. Cut the rounds into half moons. Bring a large pot of salted water to a boil, add the squash, and boil just until tender; drain.

3. Melt the ¼ cup butter in a medium Lodge cast iron skillet over medium-high heat. Add the onion, and cook until softened, stirring occasionally; add the garlic, and cook for 1 minute. Stir in the parsley, season with the salt and pepper to taste, and remove the skillet from the heat.

4. Soak the bread in ice water to cover until softened, then squeeze out the moisture and chop. Add to the onion in the pan, and cook over medium-high heat for 3 minutes, stirring occasionally. Add the squash, cook 3 minutes, stirring occasionally, and remove from the heat. Stir in the eggs, and season with the salt and pepper to taste.

5. Divide the mixture between the prepared mini servers. Sprinkle each with the crushed crackers, then dot with the pieces of butter. Bake until hot and golden brown on top, 20 to 25 minutes.

Isabelle Bishop (Mrs. Samuel Blaine Bishop), a Kellermann family friend, sent over this sweet potato dish after a death in the Kellermann family. The recipe immediately became a favorite of the family of Carolyn Kellermann Millhiser, great-granddaughter of company founder Joseph Lodge. The recipe continues to be a family favorite, and brothers William and Richard Millhiser frequently take Miss Isabelle's Sweet Potato Casserole to friends' gatherings.

SWEET POTATO CASSEROLE

Serves 5 to 8

3 cups mashed cooked sweet potatoes
1 cup granulated sugar
2 large eggs
½ cup whole milk
½ teaspoon salt
1 teaspoon vanilla extract

1 cup firmly packed light brown sugar
½ cup bleached all-purpose flour
1 cup chopped pecans
¼ cup (½ stick) salted butter or margarine, melted

1. Preheat the oven to 400°F. Grease a Lodge 3.6-quart covered enameled cast iron casserole or two Lodge 9-ounce cast iron oval mini servers.

2. In a large bowl, combine the sweet potatoes, granulated sugar, eggs, milk, salt, and vanilla. Pour into the prepared casserole or mini servers.

3. In a small bowl, combine the brown sugar, flour, pecans, and melted butter until mixed well. Sprinkle evenly over the top of the casserole. Bake until the topping browns, 30 to 40 minutes.

SUN-DRIED TOMATO-RICOTTA GNOCCHI WITH BASIL PESTO

Serves 4 to 6 as a side dish

This recipe is from George B. Stevenson, former chef de cuisine at Pearl's Foggy Mountain Café in Sewanee, Tennessee. It is a versatile and flavorful dish that is an excellent side, but one that can easily be served on its own as an entrée.

⅓ to ½ cup Basil Pesto (recipe at right)
2 ounces sun-dried tomatoes
1¼ cups all-purpose flour, plus more for rolling
1 large egg
15 ounces fresh ricotta cheese
1½ teaspoons kosher salt

½ teaspoon plus pinch of freshly ground black pepper
1 tablespoon extra virgin olive oil
1 tablespoon unsalted butter
2 tablespoons pine nuts, toasted in a 350°F oven for 5 minutes

1. Prepare the Basil Pesto.
2. Cover the sun-dried tomatoes with water in a small saucepan, and bring to a boil. Remove from the heat, and let steep for several minutes. Drain, squeeze out any excess water, and chop the tomatoes.
3. Bring a large pot of lightly salted water to a boil.
4. In the bowl of an electric stand mixer fitted with the paddle attachment, place the chopped tomatoes, flour, egg, ricotta, 1 teaspoon of the salt, and ¼ teaspoon of the pepper, and mix on low until combined and the mixture forms a loose dough. Transfer the dough to a lightly floured work surface. Cut in half, then, with lightly floured hands, roll each half into a ¾-inch-diameter log. With a bench scraper or knife, cut the logs on the diagonal into ¾-inch-thick slices.
5. Transfer the gnocchi to the boiling water, and cook until they plump up and float to the surface, 5 to 7 minutes. Using a slotted spoon or skimmer, gently transfer them to a colander to drain.

How George Makes Gnocchi

1. If the dough sticks to the work surface when rolling it into logs, sprinkle a small amount of flour onto the surface—too much will make the gnocchi heavy and dense.

2. Be sure to cut the gnocchi into equal sizes (¾ inch thick) so they'll cook evenly.

3. Boil the gnocchi in a large pot of salted water. They'll plump up and bob to the surface when they're ready to serve (5 to 7 minutes).

4. Use a slotted spoon or skimmer to remove the gnocchi from the boiling water to a colander.

6. When all the gnocchi have been cooked, heat the oil and butter together in a Lodge 15-inch cast iron skillet over medium-high heat until the butter starts to brown. Add the gnocchi, and sprinkle with the remaining ½ teaspoon salt and pinch of pepper. Allow to brown on all sides, tossing occasionally.

7. Turn off the heat, add the pesto, and toss until the gnocchi are coated. Portion the gnocchi onto plates, and sprinkle with the toasted pine nuts.

BASIL PESTO

Makes about 1 cup

- 1 cup packed fresh basil leaves
- ½ tablespoon chopped garlic
- 2 tablespoons pine nuts
- 3 tablespoons extra-virgin olive oil
- Kosher salt and freshly ground black pepper to taste
- ¼ cup grated Parmigiano-Reggiano cheese

Combine all the ingredients in a food processor; process until smooth. Will keep, tightly covered, in the refrigerator for 4 to 5 days.

Potato latkes (pancakes) are a holiday tradition in the home of Peter Kaminsky, a food and outdoors writer and cookbook author. His most recent book is *Bacon Nation*.

POTATO "LODGEKES"

Serves a bunch of people (maybe 15 or so)

- 12 large Idaho potatoes, peeled and cut into chunks
- 2 medium Spanish onions, cut into chunks
- 5 large eggs, beaten
- ½ cup matzoh meal or cracker meal

Salt (salty is good) and freshly ground black pepper
1½ cups peanut oil (peanut oil has a high smoke point and works best, but you can also use canola oil)

1. In a food processor fitted with the shredding blade, grate the potatoes. As the bowl of the food processor fills up, empty the potatoes into a large colander or sieve placed in the sink.

2. Grate the onions, and set aside in a bowl.

3. Pick up the potatoes, a handful at a time, and squeeze to remove as much liquid as possible. Place the squeezed potatoes in a bowl.

4. When all the potatoes are squeezed, put the chopping blade in the food processor, and process half of the potatoes and all of the onions into a rough puree. Empty the puree into a bowl, and, taking a handful at a time, squeeze as much liquid as possible out of the potato/onion puree. Place in the colander or sieve to continue draining for 15 to 30 minutes. You can also put the puree in cheesecloth and squeeze out the liquid that way. Don't worry if the potatoes turn brown while standing.

5. Transfer the mixture to a large bowl. Add the remaining grated potatoes, the eggs, and matzoh meal. Season with the salt and pepper, and mix well with a rubber spatula. Cover with plastic wrap, and set aside.

6. Heat the oil in a Lodge 15-inch cast iron skillet over medium-high heat until it begins to shimmer. The oil should be about ¼ inch deep. Using a large spoon, ladle the batter for two pancakes into the hot oil. Cook until golden brown, about 3 minutes, and flip. Cook 3 minutes more. Remove one and taste. The inside should be cooked through and the outside golden brown on both sides. Keep adjusting the heat and cooking time and adding more oil as you cook the rest of the pancakes, 3 or 4 at a time. Drain on paper towels before serving.

A CAST IRON MEMORY

At the Kaminskys' in Brooklyn, New York, the family picks a convenient date in the beginning of December, writes to friends, and invites them to an open house. Says Peter, "I use two big Lodge skillets." As a side dish, they often poach a lot of vegetables in white wine and olive oil and arrange them on a big platter. "Also, we put out a quart or two of pickled herring that I fetch from the ladies at Nordic Delicacies in Bay Ridge, Brooklyn. Some pals on the West Coast usually send smoked wild salmon from the Pike Place Market, and Nancy Newsom Mahaffey of Princeton, Kentucky, sends one of her amazing country hams, which ain't kosher, but it sure is good. For drinks, sparkling wine, sparkling cider, a hearty red wine, or, my favorite, a crisp ale," Peter relates. Top the individual latkes with sour cream, smoked salmon, or applesauce (or nothing).

Peter suggests, "Wear an apron when making these. Or if you are not the apron-wearing type, try overalls…or camo."

Jesse Ziff Cool is dedicated to sustainable agriculture and practices it every day in her three restaurants, Flea Street and Cool Café @ MBP in Menlo Park and Cool Café in Stanford, California. Adding parsnips and yams creates an irresistible kugel that is great on its own with a dollop of sour cream or as a side dish. The even heat from the iron skillet results in a crispy crust, which is a must in a kugel. Says Jesse, "I still use my grandmother's iron skillet. I don't think I would even consider making a kugel in any other pan."

POTATO, PARSNIP, AND YAM KUGEL

Serves 8 or more

3 tablespoons vegetable oil	6 large eggs, beaten
4 medium red- or yellow-skin potatoes	¼ cup unbleached all-purpose flour
2 medium parsnips	1½ teaspoons chopped fresh thyme
2 medium yams or sweet potatoes	1 teaspoon freshly ground black pepper
3 teaspoons kosher salt	
2 medium yellow onions, peeled	

1. Preheat the oven to 425°F. Generously oil a Lodge 10-inch cast iron skillet, and put in the oven. Save 1 teaspoon of the oil to brush on the top of the kugel before baking.

2. Peel and, using the large holes of a box grater, grate the potatoes, parsnips, and yams into a large colander. Toss with 1 teaspoon of the salt, and let drain for 15 minutes to remove excess liquid, pressing on the mixture a few times.

3. While the mixture is draining, using the large holes on the grater, grate the onions in a large bowl. When the potatoes, parsnips, and yams have finished draining, add to the onions, and toss to combine. Add the eggs, flour, thyme, pepper, and remaining 2 teaspoons salt, and mix to combine well.

4. Remove the skillet from the oven, and pour the kugel batter into the hot pan. Brush the top with the reserved 1 teaspoon oil. Reduce the oven temperature to 375°F, and bake the kugel until golden brown and tender at the center when tested with the tip of a knife, about 1 hour. Remove from the oven, and let stand for 10 minutes before cutting.

Debbie Moose, a cookbook author and freelance writer in Raleigh, North Carolina, came up with this recipe in response to a friend who doesn't like the flavor of sage, which dominates traditional holiday dressings. "The flavor of this dressing makes it elegant enough to serve year-round," Debbie says.

ROSEMARY-THYME DRESSING

Serves 6 to 8

3 tablespoons butter	¾ tablespoon chopped fresh thyme or ¾ teaspoon dried thyme
¾ cup chopped celery	
1 cup chopped onion	¼ teaspoon salt, or to taste
½ cup chopped green bell pepper	¼ teaspoon freshly ground black pepper, or to taste
6 cups cubed (½ inch) French bread	3 cups chicken broth
2½ tablespoons chopped fresh rosemary or 2½ teaspoons dried rosemary	1 large egg, lightly beaten

1. Place a Lodge 9- or 10-inch cast iron skillet in the oven; preheat the oven to 350°F while you prepare the stuffing.

2. Place 2 tablespoons of the butter in a small Lodge cast iron skillet over medium heat. Cook the celery, onion, and bell pepper, stirring, until softened but not browned.

3. Place the bread cubes in a large bowl. Stir in the vegetables, then add the rosemary, thyme, salt, and pepper. Stir to combine. Add the broth, and stir well. Let the mixture stand for a few minutes, until the bread absorbs most of the broth. Stir in the egg.

4. Place the remaining 1 tablespoon butter in the heated skillet, and swirl to coat the bottom and sides. Add the stuffing mixture. Bake until browned on top, about 1 hour.

A CAST IRON MEMORY

I use a cast iron skillet that my mother received as a wedding gift, which makes the skillet over 56 years old. After decades of frying and baking, oiling and buttering, it's as nonstick as any flashy new pan and has lasted a heckuva lot longer. In my mother's time, a cast iron skillet, a deviled egg plate, and a hand-cranked ice cream maker were standard gifts for every bride. Now, couples receive everything from toolboxes to single-serve coffee makers. Some brides might even frown if they receive a cast iron skillet and find out they can't throw it in the dishwasher with the travel mugs and microwave plates. But there is no companion in my kitchen like that skillet. Although what I cook in it is very different from my mother's recipes, it reminds me that being in the kitchen and feeding the people I love will always endure.

—Debbie Moose

During the hot "dog days" of summer, when corn was being harvested out of the gardens, the Newsom family, particularly Colonel Bill and his wife, Jane, would prepare Southern-style creamed corn, his pan-cooked aged country ham, and juicy homegrown tomatoes for an evening meal. Today, Nancy Newsom Mahaffey, owner of Newsom's Old Mill Store and Colonel Bill Newsom's Aged Kentucky Country Ham, prepares the same meal for her own family when the hot weather hits.

SOUTHERN-STYLE CREAMED CORN

Serves 12

- 12 ears fresh corn
- 2½ tablespoons stick margarine or salted butter
- 1 cup water
- 1 cup milk
- 3 heaping tablespoons sugar (optional)
- ½ teaspoon salt (optional)
- Scant ½ teaspoon freshly ground black pepper
- 3 heaping tablespoons self-rising or all-purpose flour
- ½ cup warm water

1. Shuck the corn, rinse, and remove the silks from the ears. Stand each ear in the middle of a large low-sided baking dish. Using a sharp serrated knife, shave the tips of each kernel from top to bottom all the way around the ear. Flip the knife over, and scrape the ear with the back, flat side of the knife, top to bottom all the way around. This is called "milking the ear." Discard the corncobs.

2. Slowly melt the margarine in a Lodge 10-inch cast iron skillet over low heat. Add the corn kernels with their milk to the skillet. Increase the heat to medium-high, and add the 1 cup water, milk, sugar, and salt, if desired, and pepper. Let the mixture bubble in the pan for 3 to 5 minutes, then reduce the heat to medium.

3. Meanwhile, place the flour in a coffee cup, and slowly add the warm water, stirring constantly. Turn the heat under the skillet to low, and add the flour slurry, stirring constantly. Cook, stirring, until the mixture thickens. If you like, you can add more milk or water if the mixture becomes too thick too fast. Serve hot.

In the summer, corn is so abundant that, at times, it's a struggle to keep up with the bounty. Corn pudding combines a number of things Oxford, Mississippi-based restaurateur and chef John Currence loves: the flavor of corn on the cob, the sweetness of creamed corn, and the lightness of a soufflé. It's just perfect and it goes with everything!

ROASTED CORN PUDDING

Serves 6

4 ears fresh corn with husks	¼ cup (½ stick) unsalted butter, melted
¼ cup chopped bacon	3 tablespoons masa harina
¼ cup diced yellow onion	1½ teaspoons cornstarch
1½ teaspoons minced garlic	2 tablespoons fresh thyme leaves
1 jalapeño chile, seeded and minced	1½ tablespoons sugar
¾ cup whole milk	Salt and freshly ground black pepper
¼ cup heavy cream	
3 large eggs	

1. Preheat the oven to 325°F. Place the unshucked ears of corn on the center rack of the oven, and roast for 35 minutes. Let cool until they can be handled, then cut the kernels off the cobs (about 2 cups kernels). Set aside. Discard the cobs. Grease a Lodge 12-inch cast iron skillet.

2. Cook the bacon in a medium cast iron skillet over medium heat until crisp. Remove the bacon to a paper towel to drain, reserving the drippings in the skillet.

3. Add the onion and garlic to the bacon drippings, and cook, stirring occasionally, until softened. Add the jalapeño and cook, stirring, until softened, about 1 minute. Stir in the roasted corn, and heat thoroughly.

4. In a small saucepan over medium heat, combine the milk and cream, and cook until bubbles form around the edge of the pan. Remove from the heat, and let cool briefly.

5. In a large bowl, whisk together the eggs, melted butter, masa, and cornstarch. Drizzle in the warm milk mixture, whisking constantly. Stir in the corn mixture until well blended. Stir in the thyme, sugar, and reserved bacon. Season with the salt and pepper to taste.

6. Pour the mixture into the prepared 12-inch skillet, and bake until the center is still jiggly but set, about 25 minutes.

In this recipe from Megan McCarthy, healthy lifestyle consultant, chef, and the force behind healthyeating101.com, she has added some vibrant colors to her favorite side dish, quinoa. Red quinoa has a bit of a heartier element to it than its white counterpart but is equally delicious. Paired with roasted acorn squash, this makes for a very nice comfort food side with plenty of protein, as well as a great source of fiber and potassium.

RED QUINOA WITH ROASTED ACORN SQUASH

Serves 4 to 6

- 1 acorn squash (1 to 2 pounds)
- 1 tablespoon extra virgin olive oil
- 1 cup red quinoa, rinsed under cold running water until water runs clear
- 2 cups water
- 2 tablespoons roasted walnut oil
- Fine sea salt and cracked black pepper
- 2 green onions, chopped

1. Preheat the oven to 400°F.

2. Slice the acorn squash in half, and scrape out the seeds. Brush the cut sides with the olive oil, and place, cut side down, on a Lodge 14-inch cast iron round baking pan. Bake until tender, about 45 minutes. Let cool. Peel off the skin, and discard. Cut the roasted squash into large pieces.

3. While the squash roasts, combine the rinsed quinoa and the water in a medium saucepan, and bring to a boil. Reduce the heat to a simmer, cover, and cook until the water is absorbed, about 12 minutes.

4. Transfer the cooked quinoa to a large bowl, drizzle with the walnut oil, and season with the salt and pepper to taste. Add the roasted squash and the green onions, and gently toss.

❧ BREADS ❧

Cornbread is the classic bread associated with cast iron cooking—and for good reason, cast iron produces the most delicious cornbread results. However, cast iron also turns out mouthwatering rolls, biscuits, and loaf bread, too. Here, you'll find recipes for all the above.

Lynda King Kellermann regularly made special meals for Sunday dinner after church and often served these rolls.

KENTUCKY STATE FAIR PRIZE-WINNING ROLLS

Makes 20 rolls

- 1 cup whole milk, scalded
- ⅔ cup sugar
- ⅔ cup vegetable shortening
- 1 tablespoon salt
- 1 cup mashed potatoes (mash them with some of their cooking water—they should be kind of soupy)
- 1 (¼-ounce) envelope active dry yeast
- ½ cup lukewarm water (about 110°F)
- 2 large eggs (if you'd like a lighter roll, separate the eggs and use only the whites), well beaten
- 5 to 5½ cups all-purpose flour
- Butter

1. In a large bowl, combine the scalded milk, sugar, shortening, salt, and mashed potatoes until well mixed. In a small bowl, dissolve the yeast in the lukewarm water.

2. When the milk has cooled to lukewarm, add the eggs, dissolved yeast, and enough of the flour to make a soft dough.

3. Put the dough in a bowl greased with butter. Grease the top of the dough. Cover with plastic wrap, and refrigerate overnight or up to 2 days.

4. Using your hands, form the rolls to be about 2 inches in diameter and about 1 inch high, then place them about 1 inch apart on a Lodge 14-inch cast iron round baking pan. Let them rise, uncovered, until doubled in size, about 1 hour. (You can also freeze the rolls once formed. If you do, let them thaw at room temperature for 3 hours before baking.)

5. Preheat the oven to 400°F. Bake the rolls until golden brown on top, about 20 minutes.

LODGE-KELLERMANN FAMILY MEMORIES

In 1932, Lynda King Kellermann came to South Pittsburg, Tennessee, to teach home economics and French at the high school. Elizabeth Lodge Kellermann, granddaughter of company founder Joseph Lodge, suggested her oldest brother, Dick, have a date with her new teacher, Miss King. During their courtship, Dick would throw pebbles at the bedroom window to get her to come downstairs. Lynda and Charles Richard "Dick" Kellermann, Jr., were married in June 1935 on the King farm.

FEATHER LIGHT ROLLS

Makes about 24 rolls

These campfire rolls are delicious served with butter and honey—homemade jam is tasty as well. This recipe was contributed by Sandy and Jack Wallace and Maureen Knapp of the International Dutch Oven Society.

1 tablespoon instant yeast (SAF)	2 large eggs
1¼ cups warm milk (110°F to 115°F)	3½ cups bread flour
¼ cup sugar	1 teaspoon salt
¼ cup light vegetable oil	¼ cup (½ stick) butter

1. Combine the yeast, milk, sugar, oil, and eggs in a large bowl, stirring well. Add 2½ cups of the flour, and stir well for 1 minute. While stirring, slowly add the salt. Add the remaining 1 cup flour, or as much of it as needed, to create a soft dough.

2. Turn the dough out onto a lightly floured surface, and knead for 5 minutes or strongly whack the dough with a large spoon 30 times. Shape the dough into a round, and place it into a copper, glass, or plastic bowl. (Avoid stainless steel or sheet metal bowls, as both can have a negative reaction with the yeast.) Cover the bowl with a clean cloth, place in a warm spot (but out of direct sun during hot weather), and let rise until doubled in bulk. (The warmer it is, the faster the dough will double—20 to 30 minutes at 75°F.)

3. While the dough is rising, melt the butter in a warm Lodge 12-inch cast iron camp Dutch oven (an oven with a flat lid). Spread the butter on the bottom and sides of the pot. Allow any excess butter to pool.

4. After the dough has risen, place it on a clean, lightly greased, flat surface. Shape the dough into a round ball. Pinch off a 1½- to 2-inch ball of dough; roll the piece of dough between your palms to round it up, then seal the seams. Drop the dough ball into the prepared Dutch oven. Roll it around in the butter to coat it on all sides, then place the roll seam side down, leaving a nice rounded top. Repeat with the remaining dough, arranging the rolls so they touch each other.

5. Cover the Dutch oven with a clean cloth or its lid, and place in a warm spot (but out of direct sun during hot weather). The Dutch oven should be warm, but not hot. Allow the rolls to rise until almost doubled. Depending on the temperature, it will take 20 to 40 minutes.

6. Arrange 8 coals in a ring underneath the Dutch oven, and place 16 coals on the lid (see Camp Dutch Oven Cooking, page 100); your target temperature inside is 325°F to 350°F. Let your rolls bake; it may take 25 to 40 minutes, depending on the ambient temperature. Keep in mind, every time you lift the lid to check on your rolls, you need to add 5 more minutes of cooking time. Be patient and trust your nose. When you can smell yeasty bread, the rolls are close to being done—about 5 more minutes. When it smells more like baked bread, the rolls are done.

7. The butter used earlier will allow the rolls to lift, slide, or dump out onto a cooling rack. They can be served hot out of the Dutch oven as well. Remember, the Dutch oven will keep cooking them, so the bottoms and sides may get a little crunchy if you leave them in. You can also let the rolls cool on a rack, then return them to the Dutch oven to serve and to keep warm.

❧ HOW TO BAKE BREAD IN A CAMP DUTCH OVEN ❧

Baking bread (any favorite free-form or country bread recipe will work) in a cast iron camp Dutch oven is a real taste treat. Whether rafting the Colorado, camping in the Sierras or the Alleghenys, or picnicking at a campsite, the combination of hot cast iron radiating heat from all sides, glowing coals, and fresh air contributes to a loaf similar in consistency to one baked in an enclosed outdoor oven. The crust is exceptionally thin and crisp and the interior sweetly fragrant. Cookbook author Beth Hensperger became familiar with this technique while river rafting the Stanislaus and American rivers and perfected it in her backyard. This recipe requires a camp Dutch oven (one with a flat lid) so that coals can be placed on top of it. See page 100 for additional information on camp Dutch oven cooking.

1. Grease the inside of the lid and the inside of a Lodge 12-inch cast iron camp Dutch oven (an oven with a flat lid) with butter. Line the bottom with parchment paper, if desired. Add a ball of dough at any point in its rising cycle. Cover the pot with the lid, and let the dough rise at room temperature (or outdoors but out of direct sun during hot weather) until doubled in size, about 1½ hours.

2. Burn a wood, charcoal, or combination fire until you have a good supply of coals. Sweep the coals into a shallow depression in the ground dug next to the fire, saving some larger coals. Set the Dutch oven on a grill, or balance it on three stones ½ inch above a ring of 6 to 8 evenly spaced hot coals. Place 12 to 16 larger coals directly on the pot lid around the edge and in the middle for even heat distribution from the top as well as the bottom of the pot.

3. Bake, fanning the coals periodically, until the bread is golden brown, crisp, and hollow sounding when tapped. Check the bread after 35 minutes, but it may take 45 to 50 minutes total. Please note that the handle of the Dutch oven will be very hot. Use a pair of pliers to lift the lid, and wear leather gloves to avoid burns.

4. Remove the loaf with care using oven mitts. Let it cool to just warm or room temperature; slice and serve.

With his passion for bread, Bill Ryan, founder of the Louisiana Dutch Oven Society, is always looking for different ways to create a great tasting roll. After tasting your first one of these, you will quickly be grabbing for more!

SPICY SAUSAGE AND CHEDDAR YEAST ROLLS

Makes 18 rolls

- ½ pound ground andouille or bulk Italian sausage
- 1 cup minced yellow onion
- 1 tablespoon minced jalapeño chile (remove seeds for less heat)
- 1 (¼-ounce) package active dry yeast
- 2 tablespoons sugar
- 2 tablespoons plus 1 teaspoon vegetable oil
- 2 cups warm water (about 110°F)
- 6 cups bread flour
- ¾ cup yellow cornmeal
- 2 teaspoons sea salt
- 2 cups (8 ounces) grated white Cheddar cheese

1. Brown the sausage in a Lodge 12-inch cast iron skillet over medium heat until fully cooked. Add the onion and jalapeño, and cook, stirring a few times, for 3 minutes. Transfer the mixture to a paper towel-lined plate to drain, and cool to room temperature.

2. In a small bowl, combine the yeast, sugar, and 2 tablespoons of the oil. Add the water. Mix about 4 minutes to dissolve the yeast.

3. In a large bowl, combine the flour, all but 2 tablespoons of the cornmeal, the salt, sausage mixture, and cheese. Mix until it lightly comes together, then add the yeast mixture, and mix until the dough pulls from the side of the bowl and forms a ball. Remove the dough from the bowl. Coat the bowl with the remaining 1 teaspoon oil, return the dough to the bowl, and turn it to oil all sides. Cover the bowl with plastic wrap, and let the dough rise in a warm area (70°F to 75°F) until doubled in size, about 2 hours.

4. Turn the dough onto a lightly floured work surface. Using your hands, gently roll it into a narrow loaf about 24 inches long. Cut the dough across into 18 equal pieces. With the palm of your hand, roll each piece into a round roll. Sprinkle the bottom of a Lodge 7-quart cast iron Dutch oven with the reserved cornmeal. Place the rolls in a single layer in the pot, spacing them 1 inch apart, cover with a clean cloth, and let rise for 30 minutes.

5. Preheat the oven to 350°F. Using a sharp knife, make an X on top of each roll. Bake until golden brown, about 20 minutes. Enjoy the rolls warm from the oven.

Brother Anselm Clark was a monk with a baking background, trained at the Culinary Institute of America in New Haven, Connecticut. He resided at the Marion Mission for several years across the Tennessee River from South Pittsburg, hometown of Lodge. His bread baking came to be greatly anticipated by all.

BROTHER ANSELM'S POPOVERS

Makes 12 popovers

Vegetable shortening
1 cup sifted all-purpose flour
¼ teaspoon salt

2 large eggs
1 cup milk
1 tablespoon butter, melted

1. Preheat the oven to 425°F. Grease two Lodge (6-cup) cast iron muffin pans with shortening, and place them in the oven for 10 minutes as it preheats.

2. Combine the flour and salt in a medium bowl. In a small bowl, beat the eggs until foamy; add the milk, stirring to combine. Gradually add the milk mixture to the flour mixture, stirring just until blended. Stir in the melted butter.

3. Fill the wells of the prepared muffin pans two-thirds full with the batter. Bake until browned, 32 to 35 minutes. They should have hollow centers when they come out of the oven. Turn them over, and make a slit in the bottom, and fill the centers with gravy or jelly, depending on the meal. (Or you can simply dollop the gravy or jelly on top.)

KITCHEN NOTE:

Make Popovers with Horseradish Sauce for a variation: Prepare the popovers as directed, adding a dash of Worcestershire sauce and a pinch of dillweed to the batter in Step 2. When they come out of the oven, slit them on the bottom, and fill them with Horseradish Sauce: Combine 1 cup sour cream, 2 tablespoons prepared horseradish, 1 chopped green onion, ¼ teaspoon Texas Pete hot sauce, ¼ teaspoon salt, and ¼ teaspoon freshly ground black pepper in a small bowl. Refrigerate the sauce until ready to serve.

HEAT-WAVE BREAD

Makes 1 loaf

Rose Levy Beranbaum, author of *The Bread Bible*, worked out this technique for the now ubiquitous no-knead bread (see Kitchen Note) one August day when the temperature soared to the upper 90s and she just didn't feel justified heating up the whole house in order to have homemade bread for her height-of-the-season tomato sandwiches and BLTs. "I had been meaning to try this technique for years, but this unusually intense heat wave finally spurred me into action. I was stunned and delighted by how easy it was to transition from indoor oven to outdoor gas grill," recounts Rose.

3 cups (16.5 ounces) Gold Medal Better for Bread flour, or half unbleached all-purpose and half bread flour

¼ teaspoon instant yeast
1½ teaspoons salt
1⅔ cups room-temperature water

1. In a large bowl, whisk together the flour and yeast, then stir in the salt. Add the water, and stir with your fingers or a silicone spatula just until the dry ingredients are moistened. The mixture will be sticky.

2. Cover the bowl tightly with plastic wrap, and allow to stand at around 70°F for 18 to 19 hours. (It will rise significantly and be filled with bubbles hours earlier, but it does not deflate up to 19 hours. This longer rising results in more flavor.)

3. Turn the dough out onto a well-floured surface. (Silpat is ideal because you need very little flour to keep it from sticking.) There is no need to flour the top of the dough. Pat the dough down gently, then do two business letter folds, pinching together the dough at the bottom to form a nice taut shape. (Because the dough is so moist and sticky, a bench scraper will be helpful in shaping the dough. Latex gloves will also keep the dough from sticking.) Place the dough on a piece of parchment paper or aluminum foil cut to 14 inches in diameter and sprinkled with flour. Let it rise at 80°F for 2 hours or at 70°F (which will take a little longer) until it is about 9 inches in diameter and 2 inches high and, when pressed lightly with a wet finger, fills in slowly.

4. Use heavy-duty potholders, preferably the mitten type that protect your lower arms. Place a covered Lodge 7-quart cast iron Dutch oven on the cooking grate of a gas grill while the grill preheats to high heat with the lid closed for 20 minutes. The grill will be about 550°F after 10 minutes, but the Dutch oven requires an additional 10 minutes. Place a trivet or heavy-duty rack alongside the grill.

5. Remove the Dutch oven lid. (Rose places hers back on the grill.) Transfer the Dutch oven to the trivet, and close the grill. Allow the Dutch oven to sit for about 1 minute to cool slightly. (Rose checked the temperature inside the oven with an infrared thermometer and it was 475°F.) Transfer the dough to the Dutch oven, cover with the lid, and place it back on the cooking grate in the center of the grill. Work quickly so the heat does not escape or dissipate. Turn off the two center burners. Close the grill lid.

6. Bake for 20 minutes. (With the center burners off, Rose's grill maintained a temperature of 450°F during this period.) Remove the Dutch oven lid, close the grill lid, and continue baking for 10 minutes. (The grill was 440°F for this period.)

7. Remove the bread from the Dutch oven (turn over to unmold it), and place it directly onto the cooking grate in the center of the grill. Close the grill lid, and bake for an additional 10 minutes. Turn off the burners, and allow the bread to stand in the covered grill for another 10 minutes.

KITCHEN NOTE:

No-knead bread is characteristically moist, bordering on pasty. If you prefer a slightly drier bread, as Rose does, slice the bread, and let the slices sit for about an hour on wire racks. Freeze any leftovers. When ready to serve, remove slices, and toast them very lightly to restore them to the consistency of perfectly fresh-baked bread.

MULTIGRAIN ARTISAN LOAF

Makes one (9-inch) loaf

1½ cups unbleached all-purpose
    flour, plus more as needed
    for sprinkling
2 cups lukewarm water
    (about 80°F)
⅓ cup four-grain cereal

3 tablespoons honey
2 teaspoons active dry yeast
¾ cup stone-ground whole-
    wheat flour
½ cup stone-ground rye flour
2 teaspoons kosher salt

1. Line a medium bowl with a clean tea towel, and sprinkle heavily with all-purpose flour. Set aside to use later for a mold to raise the bread.

2. In a large bowl, combine the water, four-grain cereal, and honey; let soak for 1 hour.

3. Sprinkle the yeast over the surface of the liquid, and whisk gently until it has dissolved. Let stand for 3 minutes. Add the 1½ cups all-purpose flour, the whole-wheat flour, rye flour, and salt. With a rubber spatula, mix together for 2 or 3 minutes by pulling the spatula through the dough mixture and flipping it to simulate a kneading motion. Cover the bowl with plastic wrap, and let rise at room temperature (75°F) or until the dough has doubled in size, about 2 hours.

4. Lightly sprinkle the top of the dough with all-purpose flour, and do a "baker's turn" on the dough. This is done by first releasing the dough around the edge of the bowl. Pull the dough outward, first on the right side, extending the dough out past the rim of the bowl approximately 6 inches. Bring the stretched dough back to the center of the bowl, and lay it on top. Do the same with the left side and the top and bottom portions of the dough, bringing the stretched dough back to the center each time. Then flip the dough over, and cover with plastic wrap. Let rise for another 2 hours, then do another baker's turn. Cover and let the dough rise until it has doubled in size, about another hour.

5. Transfer the dough to a floured work surface, and do one more baker's turn. Invert the loaf so it is seam side down, and gently round to tighten the loaf. Place in the towel-lined bowl with the seam side up. Cover the top of the loaf with the extended ends of the tea towel. Let rise until the loaf feels like gelatin, about 2 hours.

6. One hour before baking, preheat the oven and a Lodge 5-quart cast iron double Dutch oven to 450°F. Carefully remove the preheated pot, and invert the loaf onto the shallow side of the pot. Quickly "score" a 4-inch square about ¼ inch deep on top of the loaf, quickly cover the loaf with the larger part of the Dutch oven, and place in the oven. Bake, covered, for 30 minutes, then remove the top, and bake until the loaf is deep golden brown, another 20 minutes.

7. Remove from the oven, and let the loaf rest for 1 hour on a wire rack to cool. Enjoy simply eaten with butter, prepared as a tartine, or as a sandwich loaf.

If you want authentic artisan bakery results, Leslie Mackie, chef-owner of Macrina Bakery & Café in Seattle, Washington, recommends that you bake your bread in a Lodge cast iron double Dutch oven. With its tight-fitting lid, the pot traps the moisture inside, allowing the loaf to rise as it bakes, creating a beautiful interior texture and deep golden brown crust.

This recipe from Bill Ryan, founder of the Louisiana Dutch Oven Society, yields five mini breads, plus a larger bread. You'll need five Lodge 5-inch cast iron mini servers for this, as well as an 8-inch Dutch oven. This bread is wonderful slathered with garlic butter.

COTTAGE CHEESE DILL BREAD

Makes five (5-inch) loaves and one (8-inch) loaf

- 2 (¼-ounce) packages active dry yeast
- ½ cup warm water (about 110°F)
- 2 teaspoons plus 2 tablespoons sugar
- 2 cups small-curd cottage cheese
- 2 tablespoons minced onion
- 2 tablespoons dill seeds
- 1 tablespoon chopped fresh dill
- 1 tablespoon baking powder
- 2 teaspoons salt
- 2 large eggs
- 4 to 4½ cups all-purpose flour
- 2 tablespoons butter, melted

1. Combine the yeast, warm water, and 2 teaspoons sugar in a small bowl, and let stand 10 minutes.

2. In a large bowl, combine the cottage cheese, onion, dill seeds, chopped dill, baking powder, salt, the remaining 2 tablespoons sugar, and the eggs. Mix well using an electric stand mixer. Stir in the yeast mixture. Add the flour 1 cup at a time, mixing well after each addition. Continue mixing/kneading until the dough is smooth and elastic.

3. Turn the dough into a greased bowl, and turn once to coat it. Cover the bowl with plastic wrap, set in a warm area (70°F to 78°F), and let rise until doubled in size, 1 to 1½ hours.

4. Grease five Lodge cast iron round mini servers and one Lodge 5- or 7-quart cast iron Dutch oven. Punch down the dough, turn it out onto a lightly floured work surface, and form into a round loaf. Pinching off about 1 cup of dough at a time, form into a ball, and set in one of the prepared servers. Take the remaining dough, form into a ball, and place in the Dutch oven. Cover all of the dough with clean cloths, and let rise until doubled in size, 45 to 60 minutes.

5. Preheat the oven to 350°F. Bake the loaves until golden brown on top, about 30 minutes. Brush the tops with the melted butter, cool for 10 minutes before removing from the pans, then let the loaves cool an additional 30 minutes before slicing.

This crusty bread from Jennifer Brush, owner of The Pastry Brush, a certified home bakery in Chardon, Ohio, that provides baking classes, is delicious and so very easy to make. The very wet dough is allowed to slowly ferment at room temperature, resulting in an extremely flavorful loaf. "This is my family's favorite to eat for breakfast with an omelet or for dinner with soup," says Jennifer.

CRUSTY BACON AND CHEESE BREAD

Serves 8

- 3 cups unbleached all-purpose flour, plus more for sprinkling on dough and flouring hands (Jennifer uses King Arthur)
- 1½ teaspoons fine sea salt
- ¼ teaspoon instant yeast
- ½ pound sliced bacon, cooked until crispy, drained, and crumbled or chopped
- 2 cups (8 ounces) shredded sharp Cheddar cheese
- 1¼ cups water

1. (Jennifer likes to mix this by hand in a 4-quart lidded plastic container so that after mixing she can just pop on the lid and leave the dough on the counter to do its thing. You can easily mix this in a medium bowl and then transfer it to a glass or plastic container with a lid. Keep in mind it will increase slightly in volume.) With a rubber spatula, mix the 3 cups flour, salt, yeast, bacon, and cheese together until incorporated. Add the water, and stir until completely incorporated. The dough should be evenly wet, with no dry spots. It will look a little "shaggy" and sticky. Cover and let stand on a counter at room temperature for 18 to 24 hours. (Jennifer likes to let it ferment for a full 24 hours if there is time.)

2. Remove the container lid. Sprinkle the top of the dough with 3 tablespoons of the flour. Flour your hands well. Remove the dough from the container or bowl by scooping your hands underneath the dough and lifting it out. The dough will be wet and soft. Make a ball with the dough by gently tucking the edges of the dough underneath while slightly turning it. Place the dough on a well-floured silicone baking mat or cotton kitchen towel, sprinkle the top of the dough ball lightly with flour, and cover with a cotton kitchen towel until doubled in size, 1½ to 2 hours. After the dough has risen for about 1 hour, preheat a Lodge 4-quart cast iron Dutch oven to 440°F in the oven. Make sure the pot is covered with the lid while preheating.

3. Remove the Dutch oven from the oven after 30 minutes. Remove the ball of dough from the bowl or towel, and place it in the pot. Cover with the lid, and bake for 30 minutes. Remove the lid, and continue to bake until golden brown, about another 15 minutes. Remove the loaf from the pot as soon as it comes out of the oven. Let cool on a wire rack for at least 1 hour before slicing.

A COOKING SECRET FROM JENNIFER

Baking in a covered cast iron pot traps the steam escaping from the moist dough and results in a soft middle and a crisp and crunchy crust.

EASY DUTCH OVEN SOURDOUGH BREAD

Makes one 12-inch loaf

This recipe is from Dennis Golden, cowboy poet, PBS TV host, and master Dutch oven chef. To make this, you need sourdough starter, which must be started 4 to 5 days ahead of when you want to bake your bread. If you're in a hurry, you can buy packaged starter at most specialty food or kitchenware stores or online and follow the directions starting with Step 2.

SOURDOUGH STARTER

- 2 cups unbleached all-purpose flour
- 2½ cups warm water (about 110°F)

SOURDOUGH BREAD

- 4 to 6 cups unbleached all-purpose flour
- 1 (¼-ounce) package active dry yeast (2¼ teaspoons)
- ¼ cup lukewarm water (about 80°F)
- 2½ tablespoons corn or canola oil or melted vegetable shortening
- 2 tablespoons sugar
- 1½ teaspoons salt
- ½ teaspoon baking soda
- Nonstick cooking spray

1. Prepare the Sourdough Starter: Combine the flour and water in a large glass jar or sturdy plastic container with a tight-fitting lid. Cover tightly, and set in a warm (but not hot) place for 4 to 5 days before using.

2. Prepare the Sourdough Bread: In a large plastic or glass bowl, mix 1 cup of the sourdough starter with 4 cups of the flour. Stir in as much water as is needed to reach a mixable, semiliquid consistency. Cover and set in a 120°F oven until the mixture is active and foamy, 45 to 60 minutes or more. In a small bowl, combine the yeast with the lukewarm water to activate. Stir in the oil, sugar, salt, and baking soda. Stir this into the sourdough mixture once it gets foamy.

3. Coat the inside of a Lodge 9-quart cast iron Dutch oven with cooking spray (including the inside of the lid). Wipe with a paper towel. Set the pot in the oven, and preheat it to 120°F.

4. While the pot heats, add more flour as needed to the sourdough mixture to form a dough that is stiff enough to turn out onto a floured board. Knead and turn the dough, adding more flour as necessary, until it is stiff enough to form a round loaf and quits sticking to your hands. Don't overknead the dough; that can hamper the rising process. Transfer the dough to the prepared and preheated Dutch oven. Gently push the loaf out to the edge of the pot. It should come only halfway up the side of the Dutch oven, or even less. Cover with the lid, and place in the warm oven to rise.

5. When the dough has risen to nearly the top of the pot (after about 45 minutes), turn the oven temperature to 375°F (yes, the dough is in the oven as it is preheating), and bake until golden brown, about 1 hour and 15 or 20 minutes.

6. Turn the loaf out onto a board or towel. Let it cool a bit, then slice and enjoy.

CRAZY FOR DUTCH OVEN COOKING

Dennis Golden

Master Dutch oven chef and cowboy poet, Reno, Nevada

Cast iron has been in my family's kitchen as long as I can remember. As a child, I helped my grandmother cook sourdough pancakes in her large cast iron skillet.

But my first vivid recollection of cooking with cast iron took place about 1948 on a hunting trip in northern Nevada. I helped my father cook sage grouse in a cast iron pot with a flat bottom and rounded lid by burying it underground in sagebrush coals. After 8 hours underground, the pot was extracted with great fanfare, and I can still remember the aroma when the lid was lifted and how we feasted like thieves on that tender, succulent bird! This method of cooking is a favorite in hunting and fishing camps and is often referred to as "bean hole cooking," which is why we always called our pot the "bean pot."

I later inherited this pot and used it to cook many meals for my own family. For years, it was used almost weekly as one of our family's most prized kitchen tools. Last year, my wife and I gave it to our daughter as a wedding present.

I use cast iron frequently, because it holds heat so well and distributes it evenly. It is practically indestructible. Despite all the modern "nonstick" surfaces, cast iron continues to be superior to most, and it cleans up easily and quickly.

After all these years of cooking, my favorite cast iron recipe is, hands down, Dutch oven sourdough bread. It's not only a family favorite, but friends have come to expect it to be delivered at Christmastime as a holiday treat!

I keep plenty of the sourdough starter on hand so I can make bread on a regular basis. If you don't use all of the starter within 4 to 5 days, you'll need to replenish the starter and keep it healthy and active. For example, if you take 1 cup of starter, then add ½ cup flour and ½ cup warm water to the jar, and repeat the procedure of leaving it in a warm place for 4 to 5 days, then refrigerate until needed again. Also, if you are a sporadic bread baker, and you haven't made bread in a month, add a couple tablespoons each of flour and water to the starter, and repeat the fermenting process before refrigerating again. With this kind of care and feeding, your starter can pretty much live forever.

Lynda King Kellermann, wife of company founder Joseph Lodge's grandson, Charles Richard "Dick" Kellermann, Jr., shared with her mother, Eula Renfro King, a love for cooking for her family. Every morning, Eula made these Crisp Biscuits for breakfast on her Barren County, Kentucky, farm. She knew exactly how many sticks of wood to put into the firebox of the woodstove to bake a biscuit.

CRISP BISCUITS

Makes 6 biscuits

Vegetable oil
1 cup all-purpose flour (measured before sifting)
1 teaspoon baking powder
½ teaspoon salt
¼ teaspoon baking soda
¼ teaspoon sugar
¼ cup vegetable shortening
⅓ cup buttermilk

1. Preheat the oven to 400°F. Lightly oil a Lodge 14-inch cast iron round baking pan with the vegetable oil.
2. Sift the dry ingredients into a medium bowl. Cut in the shortening with a pastry blender until the mixture resembles coarse meal. Add the buttermilk all at once, and stir until the mixture is well dampened.
3. Turn the dough onto a lightly floured board. Roll out to ⅓- to ½-inch thickness, and cut with a 3-inch round cutter. Pat the scraps together, and cut out more biscuits. Place the biscuits ½ inch apart on the prepared baking pan. Bake until the tops are golden brown, about 15 minutes.

In the South, cathead biscuits are also called scratch biscuits, and nobody knows the real derivation of either name. One quaint explanation is that the craggy ridges look like a cat's ears; another is that the irregular tops resemble fur. In any case, cookbook author James Villas says catheads must be shaped by hand, and they are baked only in heavy cast iron skillets. For the right texture, do not substitute butter or margarine for the lard in these biscuits, and serve them with plenty of butter and fruit preserves, molasses, or sorghum syrup.

CATHEAD BISCUITS

Makes about 1½ dozen biscuits

- 3 cups all-purpose flour
- 4 teaspoons baking powder
- 1 teaspoon salt
- ½ teaspoon baking soda
- 1 cup chilled lard, cut into pieces
- 1 cup buttermilk, or as needed

1. Preheat the oven to 325°F. Grease two Lodge 12-inch cast iron skillets, and set aside.
2. In a large bowl, whisk the flour, baking powder, salt, and baking soda together. Add the lard, and cut it in with a pastry blender or rub it into the flour with your fingertips until the mixture is just crumbly. Gradually stir in just enough buttermilk to form a soft ball of dough.
3. Transfer the dough to a lightly floured work surface, knead about 8 times, then shape by hand into biscuits about 3½ inches across and 1 inch high.
4. Arrange the biscuits fairly close together in the prepared skillets, and bake in the upper third of the oven until golden brown and craggy on the outsides, about 17 minutes.

This very simple, old-fashioned recipe from Marilyn Geraldson works only with cast iron and is for all Southerners who love their biscuits. In the 1990s, Marilyn assisted in the selection of recipes to be included with Lodge bakeware.

BUTTERMILK DROP BISCUITS

Makes 7 biscuits

Vegetable shortening
2 cups all-purpose flour
1 tablespoon baking powder
2 teaspoons sugar
½ teaspoon cream of tartar
¼ teaspoon salt
¼ teaspoon baking soda
½ cup butter, margarine, or vegetable shortening
1¼ cups buttermilk

1. Preheat the oven to 450°F. Grease the wells of a Lodge cast iron mini cake pan with the shortening.
2. Stir together the dry ingredients in a medium bowl. Cut in the butter with a pastry blender or fork until the mixture resembles coarse crumbs. Add the buttermilk, and stir just until blended.
3. Drop the dough into the prepared pan. (The wells will be quite full.) Bake until browned on top, about 20 minutes.

KITCHEN NOTE:

For a variation, add 2 tablespoons finely shredded carrots, 1 tablespoon chopped fresh parsley, and/or 1 tablespoon chopped green onions when you add the buttermilk.

CORNBREAD, SAUSAGE, AND TOMATO PIE with GARLIC CREAM DRIZZLE

Serves 8

Lisa Keys from Middlebury, Connecticut, took home second prize at the 2012 National Cornbread Cook-Off with this delicious recipe. Lisa put a creative upside-down spin on her version of tomato pie made with fluffy sweet cornbread. Inverting the dish reveals the beautiful grape tomato topping.

CORNBREAD

- ½ pound sweet Italian sausages, casings removed
- 6 tablespoons extra-virgin olive oil
- 1 pint (2 cups) grape tomatoes, halved
- ½ cup chopped sweet onion
- 1 tablespoon sugar
- 1 teaspoon dried Italian seasoning
- 2 (7-ounce) packages Martha White Sweet Yellow Cornbread & Muffin Mix
- ¼ cup grated Parmesan cheese
- ½ cup milk
- ½ cup sour cream
- 3 large eggs, lightly beaten

GARLIC CREAM DRIZZLE

- ¼ cup heavy cream, plus more as needed
- 1 teaspoon Martha White Self-Rising Enriched White Corn Meal Mix or Martha White Plain Enriched Corn Meal
- 2 garlic cloves, crushed
- 2 fresh basil leaves
- ¼ cup sour cream
- 2 tablespoons grated Parmesan cheese
- ¼ teaspoon kosher salt
- ¼ teaspoon black pepper
- Shaved Parmesan cheese and fresh basil leaves, for garnish

1. Prepare the Cornbread: Preheat the oven to 375°F. Brown the sausage in a Lodge 10-inch cast iron skillet over medium heat until no longer pink, breaking up the meat with a wooden spoon. Drain on paper towels. Add 2 tablespoons of the oil to the pan, along with the tomatoes, onion, sugar, and ½ teaspoon of the Italian seasoning. Cook, stirring occasionally, until the tomatoes and onion begin to caramelize, about 8 minutes. Spread the tomato mixture evenly over the bottom of the pan. Spoon the sausage evenly over the top.

How Lisa Removes Cornbread from the Pan

1. After the cooked bread has rested for 5 minutes, place an inverted plate on top of the skillet. Gently invert the pan so that the skillet is upside down.

2. Place the plate on a flat surface, and gently lift the pan upward to remove the bread from the pan.

3. Some of the tomatoes or onions may stick to the pan; just gently scrape them off and place on top of the bread.

2. In a medium bowl, stir the cornbread mix, Parmesan, milk, sour cream, eggs, remaining 4 tablespoons oil, and remaining ½ teaspoon Italian seasoning together until smooth. Pour evenly over the mixture in the skillet. Bake until golden brown, 20 to 25 minutes. Let stand 5 minutes before inverting onto a serving plate. If any tomatoes or onions stick to the bottom of the pan, scrape them off, and replace on the cornbread.

3. Prepare the Garlic Cream Drizzle: Stir together the cream, cornmeal mix, garlic, and basil in a microwave-safe 1-cup measuring cup or bowl. Heat on HIGH in the microwave for 45 to 60 seconds or until the mixture boils. Discard the garlic and basil. In a small bowl, whisk the sour cream, Parmesan, salt, and pepper together. Add to the cream mixture. Add 1 to 2 tablespoons more cream if needed to reach a drizzling consistency.

4. Sprinkle the cornbread with the shaved Parmesan and basil leaves. Cut into wedges, and serve the Garlic Cream Drizzle on the side.

An homage to her Aunt T (see A Cast Iron Memory at left), Tamie Cook contributed This Ain't No Yankee Cornbread. Tamie is a chef, caterer, food writer, and former culinary director of Alton Brown's *Good Eats* program on the Food Network.

THIS AIN'T NO YANKEE CORNBREAD

Serves 2 (4 if you're not a real cornbread fan)

- 2 tablespoons bacon drippings
- 1 cup white cornmeal
- 1 teaspoon baking powder
- 1 teaspoon salt
- 1 large egg, lightly beaten
- 1 cup buttermilk, or more if needed

1. Place 1 tablespoon of the bacon drippings in a Lodge 6½-inch cast iron skillet; place the skillet in the oven while it preheats to 425°F.

2. Whisk together the cornmeal, baking powder, and salt in a small bowl. Whisk together the egg, buttermilk, and remaining 1 tablespoon bacon drippings in a medium bowl. Add the dry ingredients to the buttermilk mixture, and stir just until combined. (The mixture should pour like pancake batter; if not, add a little more buttermilk.)

3. Pour the batter into the hot skillet. Bake until the crust is dark golden brown, 15 to 20 minutes. Serve hot, no chaser.

CORN FINGERS

Makes 12 to 13

- ½ cup (2.25 ounces) yellow cornmeal (preferably stone-ground, such as Kenyon's)
- ½ cup plus ½ tablespoon (2.5 ounces) bleached all-purpose flour (preferably Gold Medal)
- 2 tablespoons plus 2 teaspoons sugar
- 1¼ teaspoons baking powder
- ½ teaspoon salt
- ½ to 1 teaspoon red pepper flakes, to taste
- 1 cup cooked corn, cut off the cob (2 small ears; see Kitchen Note)
- ⅓ cup heavy cream
- ⅓ cup whole milk
- ¼ cup (2 ounces) unsalted butter, melted
- 1 large egg yolk
- 1 large egg white

1. At least 20 minutes before baking, preheat the oven to 425°F. Position the rack in the center of the oven. Lightly grease two Lodge cast iron corn stick pans with nonstick cooking spray or oil. Five to ten minutes before the batter is ready, preheat the molds in the oven.

2. Stir the cornmeal, flour, sugar, baking powder, salt, and red pepper in a medium bowl. Add the corn; stir until coated with the mixture.

3. In a 2-cup glass measuring cup or bowl, lightly whisk together the cream, milk, melted butter, and egg yolk.

4. In a medium bowl, beat the egg white with an electric mixer until soft peaks form when the beater is lifted slowly.

5. Stir the cream mixture into the flour mixture just until moistened. There will still be lumps. Fold in the beaten egg white just until incorporated. You should still see little lumps.

6. Spoon or pipe the batter into the hot molds, almost to the top of each depression. Use a small metal spatula or the back of a teaspoon to smooth the batter, if necessary. If piping, use a pastry bag with a plain ½-inch-wide tube. Fill any empty depressions in the mold half full with water. Bake the corn fingers until the tops are golden brown, about 15 minutes.

7. Unmold the corn fingers; loosen the sides of each finger with a small metal spatula. Place a wire rack over one mold, and invert so that they are all supported by the rack. Repeat with the second mold. These corn fingers are wonderfully tender, so they require care while still warm to avoid breaking them. Serve warm or at room temperature. They also freeze well, up to several weeks. Let cool completely, then wrap each one airtight in plastic wrap, and place in heavy-duty zip-top freezer bags. To reheat from frozen, bake in a preheated 400°F oven for 7 minutes.

KITCHEN NOTE:

To cook the corn, boil it in unsalted water until just tender when pierced with a cake tester or skewer, 5 to 7 minutes. Fresh corn needs to be cooked in order to remove some of its moisture; otherwise it would make the batter too liquid.

These corn fingers, baked in a corn finger mold to resemble little individual corn on the cobs, are tender, fine-grained, and slightly sweet with little nubbins of corn in each bite and the glad surprise of occasional hot pepper flakes. They seem to dissolve in the mouth yet have a full corn flavor. Rose Levy Beranbaum makes these every summer when Jersey corn is in season. She also sometimes makes them in the winter, when she has the craving, and resorts to canned corn "niblets," which she finds to have the best flavor and texture of any processed corn kernels. This recipe is adapted from her cookbook *The Bread Bible*.

❧ DESSERTS ❧

When company's coming or you're celebrating
a special occasion, or when you're simply
craving something sweet, reach for these
recipes. Dutch Oven Danish Cake, Apple-
Cranberry Pie, Gooey Chocolate Skillets, and
Gluten-Free Rhubarb-Millet Crisp are just a
taste of the sugary fixes this chapter offers.

"This recipe was handed down from my great-grandmother to my grandmother, to my mother, to me," says Billie Jobyna Cline Hill, who worked as a secretary at Lodge for almost 60 years. "My grandmother made notes in the margin about using only cast iron for the icing." Double the icing recipe if you would like to ice the top and side of the cake instead of just using it as a filling.

JULIA CLINE'S JAM CAKE

Makes one 3-layer (10-inch) cake

- ½ cup (1 stick) salted butter, melted
- 2 cups sugar
- 6 large egg yolks
- 2 cups buttermilk
- 2 teaspoons baking soda
- 3 cups all-purpose flour
- 3 tablespoons unsweetened cocoa powder (Billie uses Hershey's)
- 2 teaspoons ground cinnamon
- 2 teaspoons ground cloves
- 2 teaspoons ground nutmeg
- 2 teaspoons ground allspice
- 2 cups jam (Billie usually makes it with blackberry)
- 1 cup dark raisins

ICING

- 1 cup whole milk
- 2 cups sugar
- ½ cup (1 stick) salted butter
- Pinch of baking soda

1. Preheat the oven to 325°F. Place a Lodge 10-inch cast iron skillet on a sheet of wax paper, and draw the outline of the bottom of the skillet. Repeat with two more sheets of wax paper. Cut out the circles, and fit into the bottoms of three Lodge 10-inch cast iron skillets. (If you have only two skillets, you can bake two layers together, then bake the last layer once they come out of the oven.) This is necessary, as the cake has a tendency to stick because of the jam.

2. In a large bowl, beat the melted butter and sugar together. Add the egg yolks, one at a time, beating well after each addition. Set aside. In another bowl, mix the buttermilk and baking soda together; let it rise for 4 minutes, then mix well. Whisk the flour, cocoa, and spices together. Add the flour mixture to the butter mixture alternately with the buttermilk mixture, mixing well. Stir in the jam and raisins. Divide the batter evenly among the three prepared skillets. Bake until a wooden pick inserted into the center of each cake comes out clean, 30 minutes. Unmold immediately after removing from the oven. Peel off the wax paper.

3. Prepare the Icing: Combine the milk, sugar, butter, and baking soda in a Lodge 5-quart cast iron deep skillet (it must be cast iron or the icing won't turn out). Cook over medium heat until the temperature of the mixture reaches the hard-ball stage on a candy thermometer, 20 to 25 minutes.

4. Set one cake layer on a cake plate. Smooth one-third of the icing over the layer. Set another layer on top of the icing, and smooth one-third of the icing over it. Top with the final cake layer, and smooth the remaining icing over it.

After a long day of enjoying the outdoors, you can knock everyone's socks off by serving this showstopper of a cake. International Dutch Oven Society members Melissa and Rebecka Boyer contributed this recipe.

DUTCH OVEN DANISH CAKE

Makes one (12-inch) layer cake; serves 10 to 12

CAKE

- 3 cups cake flour
- 4 teaspoons baking powder
- ½ teaspoon salt
- ¾ cup vegetable shortening
- 1¾ cups granulated sugar
- 1 cup milk
- 1 teaspoon vanilla extract
- ½ teaspoon almond extract
- 5 large egg whites

TOPPING

- 1 (4¾-ounce) package strawberry-flavored Danish dessert mix (such as Junket Danish Dessert)
- 2 cups confectioners' sugar
- 1 (16-ounce) tub Cool Whip
- 1 (8-ounce) package cream cheese
- 1 pound fresh strawberries, hulled

1. Grease two Lodge 12-inch cast iron camp Dutch ovens (ovens with flat lids).

2. Prepare the Cake: Sift and measure the flour into a medium bowl. Add the baking powder and salt, and sift again. In a large bowl, beat the shortening with an electric mixer. Gradually add the granulated sugar and beat until fluffy. Add the flour mixture to the shortening mixture alternately with the milk and extracts. Beat until blended after each addition.

3. In another large bowl, beat the egg whites with an electric mixer until stiff peaks form; gently fold into the batter until no white streaks remain. Divide the batter between the prepared Dutch ovens, and bake with 8 coals evenly arranged underneath each oven and 17 coals on top of the lids of each oven (see Camp Dutch Oven Cooking, page 100; 350°F). Cook until a wooden pick inserted into the center of each comes out clean, 25 to 30 minutes.

4. Prepare the Topping: While the cakes cool, make the Danish dessert following the package directions for the pie glaze.

5. Flip the cakes out of the Dutch ovens onto their lids. Stir together 1 cup of the confectioners' sugar with the Cool Whip. In a separate bowl, beat together the remaining 1 cup confectioners' sugar and the cream cheese. Combine the cream cheese and Cool Whip mixtures. Spread about half the Cool Whip mixture on the top of one of the cakes. Arrange half the strawberries on top. Place the other cake layer on top, and spread the remaining Cool Whip mixture over the cake layer. Arrange the remaining strawberries attractively over the topping, and spread the topping over the strawberries.

GRANDMOTHER'S APPLE CAKE

Serves 8

San Francisco-based pastry chef Emily Luchetti collects cast iron pans to cook in her wood-fired oven, including many vintage pieces. Says Emily, "It's the one antique you can use and not worry about breaking!"

This recipe comes from her father-in-law's grandmother, who made it for him over 75 years ago. Baking the cake in a cast iron pan gives it a delicious brown bottom, but be careful not to overcook it or it will be dry. The cake is best warm, but it can be made a day in advance; wrap in plastic wrap, and store at room temperature. Reheat in a 350°F oven for 5 minutes.

- 9 tablespoons sugar
- 1 cup all-purpose flour
- ½ teaspoon salt
- 1 teaspoon baking powder
- 1 large egg
- 2 tablespoons milk
- 1 teaspoon vanilla extract
- ¼ cup (½ stick) unsalted butter, softened
- 3 medium Golden Delicious apples
- ½ teaspoon ground cinnamon
- Chantilly Cream (recipe follows)

1. Preheat the oven to 400°F. Coat the bottom of a Lodge 10-inch cast iron skillet with cooking spray. Sprinkle 2 tablespoons of the sugar over the bottom of the pan.

2. In a small bowl, sift the flour, salt, and baking powder together. In another small bowl, whisk the egg, milk, and vanilla together.

3. In a large bowl, cream the butter and 4 tablespoons of the sugar together until light, about 1 minute with a stand mixer or 2 minutes with a handheld mixer. By hand, stir in one third of the flour mixture and then one third of the milk mixture just until mixed. Add the remaining flour and milk mixtures in two more additions. Spread the batter in the prepared skillet. It will be thick and a little sticky. If difficult to spread, wet the back of a spoon or your fingertips to push the batter out to the edge.

4. Peel and core the apples. Cut them into slices ⅛ inch thick. Starting from the outer edge of the cake, arrange the slices in concentric circles, slightly overlapping, over the top of the batter, completely covering it. In a small bowl, mix the remaining 3 tablespoons sugar with the cinnamon, and sprinkle it over the apples.

5. Bake until a wooden pick inserted in the center of the cake comes out clean, 20 to 25 minutes. Do not overcook or the cake will be dry. Let cool on a wire rack for 10 minutes. Loosen the edge and bottom of the cake from the pan using a large metal spatula. Place a large plate on top of the cake. Invert the pan and plate together, then remove the pan. Place another plate on top of the cake, and invert it again so it is right side up. Serve with Chantilly Cream.

CHANTILLY CREAM

Makes 2 cups

- 1 cup heavy (whipping) cream
- 3 tablespoons sugar
- ½ teaspoon vanilla extract

Combine all the ingredients in a medium bowl, and beat with an electric mixer on medium-high speed until soft peaks form. Refrigerate until you are ready to use. This can be made a couple of hours in advance. It may thin out, especially near the bottom. If it does, whisk briefly to thicken.

Lifestyle expert Ross Sveback developed this recipe especially for use with the Lodge cast iron mini cake pan. "I love the combination of lemon and lavender," Ross says. He suggests splitting the pound cakes open, filling them with fresh berries, and topping with lightly whipped cream, as you would shortcakes. If you don't grow your own lavender, you can purchase culinary lavender from Dean & Deluca at deandeluca.com.

LEMON-LAVENDER POUND CAKES

Makes 7 individual pound cakes

- 2 lemons
- 1½ cups sugar, preferably superfine
- 1½ cups cake flour (whisk it first before measuring to "sift" it)
- ¼ teaspoon baking soda
- ¼ teaspoon salt
- 2 tablespoons dried lavender buds
- ½ cup (1 stick) unsalted butter, at room temperature
- 3 large eggs
- ½ cup sour cream (regular, not light), at room temperature
- 1 teaspoon lemon extract (not lemon oil)
- Lavender sprigs for garnish (optional)

1. Preheat the oven to 325°F. Prepare a Lodge cast iron mini cake pan by coating it with cooking spray and lightly flouring it (Ross uses Bak-klene, a nonstick spray that contains starch, so you can skip the flouring part).

2. Zest the lemons, and place the zest in a large bowl with the sugar. Juice the lemons into a liquid measuring cup.

3. Combine the flour, baking soda, salt, and lavender buds in a medium bowl.

4. Add the butter to the sugar. Using an electric mixer on medium speed, cream them together, making sure to scrape down the bowl so that it is fully combined. Add the eggs, one at a time, beating well after each addition. Reduce the speed to low, and add the dry ingredients all at once, beating until well blended. Add the sour cream, lemon extract, and lemon juice, beating until blended.

5. Divide the batter between the wells of the prepared mini cake pan, and bake until a wooden pick inserted in the center of each comes out clean, 20 to 25 minutes. Let the cakes cool in the pan on a wire rack for 5 minutes. Remove the cakes from the pan, and place on the rack until you are ready to serve. Garnish with the lavender, if desired.

Cookbook author and baking expert Julie Hasson loves using her cast iron skillet to bake pie—there's something satisfyingly old-fashioned about it. This pie has no bottom crust, which makes it quick to prepare, perfect for a last-minute dessert. Try it topped with a scoop of ice cream.

BLUEBERRY-PEACH SKILLET PIE

Serves 6

FILLING

- 5 cups frozen blueberries (don't thaw)
- ⅔ cup granulated sugar
- ¼ cup plus ⅔ cup water
- ¼ cup cornstarch
- Grated zest from 1 lemon
- 2 ripe medium peaches, peeled, pitted, and sliced (see Kitchen Note)

TOPPING

- ¾ cup unbleached all-purpose flour
- ½ cup old-fashioned rolled oats (don't use quick cooking)
- ½ cup firmly packed light brown sugar
- 1 teaspoon freshly grated nutmeg
- ¼ cup nonhydrogenated margarine (such as Earth Balance), melted
- Ice cream for serving (optional)

1. Preheat the oven to 400°F. Lightly grease a Lodge 10-inch cast iron skillet with a little shortening.

2. Prepare the Filling: In a large saucepan, combine the blueberries, granulated sugar, and ¼ cup of the water. Bring to a simmer over medium heat, stirring occasionally.

3. Whisk together the cornstarch and remaining ⅔ cup water in a small bowl until smooth. Stir the cornstarch mixture into the hot berries. Gently stir in the lemon zest and peaches, being careful not to mash the peaches. Reduce the heat to low, and continue simmering the fruit, gently stirring, until the juices have thickened and the mixture is clear. Remove the saucepan from the heat, and scoop the mixture into the prepared skillet.

4. Prepare the Topping: Stir together the flour, oats, brown sugar, and nutmeg in a small bowl. Add the melted margarine, stirring until incorporated. Using your fingertips, work the margarine into the flour mixture, squeezing until nice and crumbly. Sprinkle the topping over the blueberry filling.

5. Bake the pie just until the topping is nicely browned, 30 to 40 minutes. Serve with the ice cream, if desired.

KITCHEN NOTE:

For an all-blueberry version, omit the peaches and increase the blueberries to 6 cups.

APPLE-CRANBERRY PIE

Makes one (9-inch) pie

- 8 ounces all-purpose flour (about 1½ cups plus 2 tablespoons)
- 1 tablespoon sugar
- ½ teaspoon salt
- ½ cup (1 stick) cold butter, cut into ¼-inch pieces
- 2 tablespoons vegetable shortening
- 2 tablespoons ice water, plus more as needed

- 2 cups fresh or frozen cranberries, picked over for stems
- 1½ cups sugar
- 4 tablespoons cornstarch
- 2 tablespoons water
- 5 cups cored, peeled, and sliced Granny Smith apples (5 medium)
- ½ teaspoon ground cinnamon
- ¼ teaspoon ground nutmeg

This is from the recipe box of Bill Ryan, founder of the Louisiana Dutch Oven Society. This recipe won Bill his third Louisiana State Dutch Oven Cook-Off in 2011.

1. In a large bowl, sift the flour, sugar, and salt together. Using your fingertips, work the butter and shortening into the flour until the mixture resembles coarse crumbs. Add the ice water, and work it in with your fingertips until incorporated and the dough comes together. Add 1 tablespoon of water at a time as needed to make a smooth dough, being careful not to overwork it. Form the dough into a disk, wrap in plastic, and refrigerate for at least 30 minutes.

2. Combine the cranberries, 1 cup of the sugar, 1 tablespoon of the cornstarch, and the water in a medium, heavy saucepan. Bring to a boil over high heat, boil for 5 minutes, remove from the heat, and let cool 15 minutes.

3. In a large bowl, combine the apples, the remaining ½ cup sugar and 3 tablespoons cornstarch, the cinnamon, and nutmeg, tossing until the apples are well coated. Stir in the cranberry mixture.

4. Take a piece of parchment paper, and cut out a circle that will fit into the bottom of a Lodge 10-inch cast iron camp Dutch oven (an oven with a flat lid). Cut five strips of parchment paper 1½ inches wide. Position them so they all cross in the center of the bottom of the Dutch oven and run up the side of the oven all around. You can fasten them in place using clothespins. Fit the parchment circle in the bottom of the oven on top of the strips. Spray the inside of the oven with cooking spray.

5. Divide the dough in half. On a lightly floured work surface, roll out one half to fit the bottom and go 1½ to 2 inches up the side of the Dutch oven. Spoon the filling into the crust. Roll out the other half of the dough so it is large enough to cover the top of the pie in the Dutch oven. Trim the crusts, then crimp the top and bottom crusts together to seal. Cut four 1-inch slits through the top crust to vent the pie while cooking. Put the lid on the Dutch oven. Set the oven on 9 coals, and set 18 coals on top of the lid (see Camp Dutch Oven Cooking, page 100; 425°F). Bake until the crust is golden brown, 40 to 50 minutes. When the pie is done, remove the lid and coals, and remove the pot from the coals. Let the pie cool for 10 minutes; lift the pie out of the oven by the parchment strips onto a serving plate. Cool completely before slicing.

KITCHEN NOTE:

If the edges of the pie start to brown too much during baking, cover them with aluminum foil.

When peaches are ripe and juicy, this divine tart from Christy Rost, cookbook author and host of the public television series *A Home for Christy Rost*, goes together quickly and looks fabulous in a cast iron skillet—perfect for your next picnic or casual gathering. A dash of Saigon cinnamon in the filling imparts a delicate, spicy flavor to the fruit. Purists may want to peel the peaches first, but leaving the skin on saves preparation time, adds extra nutrition and texture, and provides a homey note to this spectacular dessert.

RUSTIC SPICED PEACH TART WITH ALMOND PASTRY

Makes one (10-inch) tart

PASTRY

- ⅓ cup sliced almonds
- 1½ cups all-purpose flour
- 1 tablespoon granulated sugar
- ¾ teaspoon salt
- ½ cup (1 stick) cold unsalted butter, cut into 8 pieces
- 3 to 4 tablespoons ice water
- ¼ teaspoon almond extract

FILLING

- 8 to 9 large peaches (about 2¾ pounds), pitted and sliced about ½ inch thick
- ¾ cup granulated sugar
- 1½ tablespoons cornstarch
- ¼ teaspoon ground Saigon cinnamon
- 1 large egg
- 1 tablespoon water
- 1 tablespoon turbinado or granulated sugar

1. Toast the almonds: Preheat the oven to 300°F. Scatter the almonds in a single layer on a baking sheet, and bake, stirring occasionally, until golden brown, about 15 minutes. Remove from the oven, and cool completely.

2. Prepare the Pastry: Process the toasted almonds in a blender or food processor until finely chopped. Add the flour, granulated sugar, and salt, and pulse to combine. Add the butter, and pulse until it resembles small peas. Add the ice water, 1 tablespoon at a time, and almond extract, and process just until the dough comes together and forms a ball around the blades. (Do not overprocess.) Remove the dough from the processor, wrap it in plastic wrap, and chill at least 30 minutes or overnight (or freeze up to 2 months).

3. Place a rack in the upper third of the oven, and preheat to 375°F.

4. Prepare the Filling: Place the peach slices in a large bowl. In a small bowl, stir together the granulated sugar, cornstarch, and cinnamon until well blended. Add the sugar mixture to the peaches, stirring gently.

5. Turn the dough out onto a floured pastry cloth or surface, and roll into a 16-inch circle using a floured rolling pin. Fold it in half, transfer to an ungreased Lodge 10-inch cast iron skillet, and gently unfold the pastry, fitting it into the bottom of the pan and allowing the excess pastry to hang over the edge. (Don't bother to trim the dough—any unevenness adds to the rustic quality of the tart.)

6. Spoon the peach mixture into the pastry, mounding it in the middle. Gently fold the edges of the pastry up around the filling, overlapping them in soft folds. Take care that the pastry doesn't tear around the edge of the tart or the juices will escape during baking.

7. Whisk together the egg and water in a small bowl. Brush the egg wash over the pastry, and sprinkle it with the turbinado sugar. Bake until the pastry is golden brown and the fruit is hot and bubbly, 35 to 40 minutes. Let cool for 1 hour to set the juices and serve warm.

GLUTEN-FREE RHUBARB-MILLET CRISP

Serves 6

- 4 cups trimmed fresh rhubarb stalks, cut into 1-inch pieces
- 1 cup granulated sugar
- Grated zest and juice of 2 large oranges
- ¼ teaspoon orange blossom water
- ½ cup millet flour
- ½ cup certified gluten-free oats (use quinoa flakes if you cannot tolerate oats)
- ⅓ cup coconut sugar (see Kitchen Note)
- ½ teaspoon kosher salt
- ½ cup (1 stick) cold unsalted butter, cut into 1-inch pieces

1. Preheat the oven to 375°F.

2. In a large bowl, toss the rhubarb, granulated sugar, orange zest and juice, and orange blossom water together until well combined. Pour the mixture into a Lodge 9-inch cast iron skillet.

3. In a medium bowl, combine the millet flour, oats, coconut sugar, and salt. Whisk to aerate the mixture. Add the cold butter, and use your fingertips to rub it into the flour, breaking the butter down into lima bean-sized pieces. Crumble this topping over the rhubarb, covering it completely.

4. Bake until the fruit is bubbling hot and the crisp topping is golden brown, about 1 hour.

KITCHEN NOTE:

If you can't locate coconut sugar, substitute firmly packed brown sugar.

There's no reason to miss warm fruit desserts when you have to give up gluten. In fact, here's a little-known secret from Shauna Ahern, the Gluten-Free Girl: You don't need gluten for most baked goods. Use a whole-grain flour like millet, with its slightly nutty taste, mix it with rhubarb and orange, and bake to bubbly brown in your favorite cast iron skillet. You can find orange blossom water, coconut sugar, and millet at most natural foods stores, gourmet markets, or online.

How Shauna Makes a Crisp

1. Before incorporating the dry ingredients with the butter, mix them together.

2. Gently rub the butter into the dry ingredients mixture with your fingertips so that small lima bean-sized pieces are formed. Be sure to start with cold butter right from the fridge so that the topping won't become overmixed.

3. With your hands, sprinkle the topping over the rhubarb mixture in the skillet, making sure the fruit mixture is completely covered.

Before the earnest heat of summer sets in, a cold snap happens in Tennessee called blackberry winter; the old timers say the colder the snap, the sweeter the berries. Jane Gaither, who blogs at *Gourmet Gadget Gal*, says "My family homeplace at the edge of the Smoky Mountains is covered with raspberry and blackberry brambles, and we pick, can, freeze, and eat them year-round." Her berry cobbler recipe uses raspberries but you can use any type of berry or peaches. Be sure to serve it warm with vanilla ice cream.

SIMPLE BERRY SKILLET COBBLER

Serves 6 to 8

- 1 (10-ounce) package frozen raspberries or 1 pint fresh berries
- 1 cup granulated sugar
- ½ cup firmly packed brown sugar
- ½ cup plus 2 tablespoons all-purpose flour
- 2 tablespoons fresh lemon juice
- ½ teaspoon ground nutmeg
- ¼ cup (½ stick) butter
- ¾ teaspoon baking powder
- ¼ teaspoon salt
- ½ cup milk

1. Place a Lodge 10-inch cast iron skillet in the oven, and preheat the oven to 350°F.

2. Stir together the raspberries, ½ cup granulated sugar, brown sugar, 2 tablespoons of the flour, lemon juice, and nutmeg in a medium bowl.

3. Melt the butter in the skillet in the oven until it starts to brown around the edge and foam. It's important to have the butter sizzling hot!

4. While the butter is melting, stir together the remaining ½ cup flour and granulated sugar, the baking powder, salt, and milk in a large bowl, just until combined. The batter may still have a few lumps, but it should be about the consistency of pancake batter.

5. Pour the batter over the butter in the hot skillet. Do not stir. Immediately spoon the berry mixture on top of the batter. Bake until the crust looks golden and crisp, 30 to 35 minutes.

Food journalist and photographer Susan Benton, owner of 30AEATS.com, says, "Living on Route 30A in the Florida Panhandle in the summertime means beach picnics, sweet corn, an abundance of blueberries, and ripe, fresh tomatoes." This recipe for blueberry cobbler, like a good cast iron skillet, Susan says, "was handed down to me by my mother, who got it from her aunt, and so on. Everyone in my family seems to have this recipe tucked away for safekeeping!"

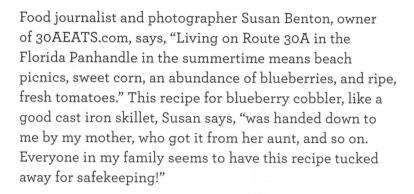

FLORIDA BLUEBERRY COBBLER

Serves 6

¼ cup (½ stick) unsalted butter, melted	2 cups fresh blueberries, picked over for stems, rinsed, and patted dry
1¼ cups sugar	Vanilla bean ice cream, for serving
1 cup self-rising flour	
1 cup whole milk	

1. Place the butter in a Lodge 10-inch cast iron skillet, and put in the oven while it preheats to 400°F.

2. In a medium bowl, whisk 1 cup of the sugar with the flour and milk until smooth.

3. Remove the skillet from the oven, and swirl the butter to evenly coat the bottom and sides. Pour the batter into the skillet, and sprinkle the blueberries evenly over the top. Sprinkle over the remaining ¼ cup sugar.

4. Bake until golden brown and bubbly, 45 minutes to 1 hour. Serve warm, topped with a dollop of ice cream.

For Tanya Holland, cookbook author and chef-owner of Brown Sugar Kitchen in Oakland, California, this dish is a celebration of her cooking experiences. "My paternal grandmother in Virginia always fried apples in a cast iron skillet. My maternal grandmother in Louisiana always toasted pecans in her pan. Cherry clafoutis was one of the first 'exotic' desserts I made when I was taking cooking classes at Peter Kump's New York Cooking School. At 23, I felt so sophisticated just being able to pronounce it!"

APPLE-PECAN CLAFOUTIS

Serves 6 to 8

¾ cup pecan pieces
1½ pounds firm, semisweet apples, like Fuji or Pink Lady
¼ cup (½ stick) unsalted butter
1 cup granulated sugar
¼ teaspoon ground cinnamon
4 large eggs
1 cup whole milk
1 tablespoon apple brandy
1½ teaspoons vanilla extract
Pinch of salt
2 cups unbleached all-purpose flour
Powdered sugar (optional)

1. Preheat the oven to 375°F. Pulse the pecans in a food processor until finely chopped; be careful not to process into a powder. Set aside.

2. Peel and core the apples. Slice the apples in half, then cut each half into ⅛-inch-thick half moons.

3. Heat a Lodge 10-inch cast iron skillet over medium heat; add the butter. When melted, swirl to coat the bottom. Add the apples, ¼ cup of the sugar, and the cinnamon, and cook until the apples soften, about 10 minutes, stirring a few times.

4. While the apples cook, whisk the eggs, remaining ¾ cup sugar, milk, brandy, and vanilla together in a medium bowl. Whisk in the pecans and salt, then slowly whisk in the flour to avoid lumps. Pour the batter over the apples in the pan. Bake for 10 minutes at 375°F, then reduce the oven temperature to 350°F, and cook until the clafoutis is nicely puffed up and browned on top, another 35 minutes. Dust with the powdered sugar, if desired. Serve immediately.

SKILLET PUMPKIN BREAD PUDDING WITH MAPLE PRALINE SAUCE

Serves 8

Portia Belloc Lowndes, director of Project FEAST, Inc. (a special events company specializing in food events), co-founder of Slow Food Chicago, and executive board member of Chicago Green City Market, prepares this recipe for her family at their century-old cabin in the northern woods of Wisconsin for Thanksgiving. She loves making it with her young daughters, as they can take part in many of the tasks, from ripping up the bread to breaking the eggs.

PUMPKIN BREAD PUDDING

- 1 cup heavy cream
- ½ cup whole milk
- ½ cup apple juice
- 6 cups torn-up French bread (about 1 loaf)
- 2 tablespoons unsalted butter, softened
- 4 large eggs
- 1 cup firmly packed light brown sugar
- 1 (15-ounce) can pumpkin puree
- ¼ cup honey
- 1 teaspoon ground cinnamon
- 1 teaspoon ground ginger
- ½ teaspoon ground nutmeg
- 2 teaspoons vanilla extract
- 1 cup raisins or sweetened dried cranberries
- ½ cup chopped pecans

MAPLE PRALINE SAUCE

- ¾ cup pure maple syrup
- ¼ cup firmly packed light brown sugar
- ¼ teaspoon salt
- ½ cup heavy cream
- ½ cup chopped pecans
- ¼ cup (½ stick) unsalted butter, cut into tablespoons

1. Prepare the Pumpkin Bread Pudding: In a measuring cup, combine the cream, milk, and apple juice. Put the torn-up bread in a large bowl, and pour the cream mixture over it. Let it all soak for about 30 minutes, stirring occasionally.

2. Preheat the oven to 375°F. Butter the bottom and sides of a Lodge 12-inch cast iron skillet with the softened butter. In a medium bowl, whisk the eggs, brown sugar, pumpkin, honey, spices, and vanilla together, then stir in the raisins and pecans. Pour the pumpkin mixture over the soaked bread, and stir to blend. Pour the mixture into the prepared skillet, and bake until set, 45 to 60 minutes.

3. While the bread pudding bakes, prepare the Maple Praline Sauce: In a heavy, medium saucepan, combine the maple syrup, brown sugar, salt, and cream, and cook over low heat, stirring until the sugar dissolves. Raise the heat to high, and bring to a boil. Let boil until the mixture thickens and reaches 220°F on a candy thermometer, stirring constantly. Stir in the pecans and butter until the butter is fully incorporated. Remove from the heat. You can use this sauce warm or cold. It will keep, tightly covered, in the refrigerator up to 1 week.

4. Serve the bread pudding drizzled with the Maple Praline Sauce.

Cookbook author and cooking instructor Rebecca Lang uses any excuse to serve dessert. She loves that with these little skillets, there's no need to share. Her warm and rich chocolate creations are as comforting as they are dreamy.

GOOEY CHOCOLATE SKILLETS

Serves 6

1 (9-ounce) package chocolate wafers (such as Nabisco Famous Chocolate Wafers)	¾ cup sugar
	⅓ cup all-purpose flour
	1½ teaspoons vanilla extract
¾ cup (1½ sticks) unsalted butter	2 large eggs, beaten
¾ cup bittersweet chocolate chips (60% cacao)	Vanilla ice cream, for serving

1. Preheat the oven to 325°F.

2. Process the wafers in a food processor fitted with the metal blade until crushed, or seal them in a zip-top plastic bag, and crush with a rolling pin. Melt ¼ cup (½ stick) of the butter in a medium saucepan. Add to the wafers; pulse to combine, or work into the crumbs with your fingertips. Press the wafer mixture into the bottom of six Lodge 5-inch cast iron skillets.

3. Melt the remaining ½ cup (1 stick) butter and the chocolate chips together in the same saucepan over low heat. Remove from the heat, and whisk in the sugar, flour, and vanilla. While whisking, add the eggs, and beat well. Divide the mixture evenly between the prepared skillets. Bake for 18 minutes (they will not look set at this point). The centers will be slightly gooey. Do not overbake.

4. Serve warm topped with a scoop of vanilla ice cream.

A COOKING SECRET FROM REBECCA

This simple fudgy dessert gets its rich, intense chocolate flavor from bittersweet chocolate chips, so it's important to use high-quality chocolate—one with at least 60% cacao.

THE GREATEST INHERITANCE

Rebecca Lang

Cookbook author and cooking instructor, Athens, Georgia

Some women inherit land, some grand diamonds, others are left with nothing more than memories. Along with a lifetime's worth of recollections of tastes and aromas in the kitchen, I inherited my grandmother Tom's prized cast iron skillet. It's well over 100 years old, yet it finds a modern home on my stainless steel stove on most days.

Skillets fall into the same category as fine china, heavy sterling silver, and family linens. They are made to pass down from generation to generation. Respecting the skillet is quintessentially honoring the previous generation. Tom cooked for so many years in this pan; it's pitch-black in color and as shiny as polished granite.

I watched Tom cook her fried chicken perfectly, complete with a browned "kiss" from the skillet after the first turn of the meat. Of all the things I remember about her kitchen, where the tools were kept and Southern staples stored, I can't recall the skillet ever being put away. It was on the stove and in the oven so much, I don't think that it ever needed a designated spot in the cabinet. It was this skillet filled with fried chicken that first taught me how comfort and love could be tasted and shared without saying a word.

On days that I miss her, which is more often than not, I simply have to wrap my fingers around the handle of her skillet and I instantly feel she's not far away. It's amazing how iron mined from far beneath the ground has bridged a gap between the lives of two cooks who loved each other dearly. I know she loved her cast iron pan, and she knew I loved her. Tom was completely at ease with it on the stove heated to crazy-high temps with hot grease sizzling away. She could turn out a batch of cornbread in it with her eyes closed. She was a woman who was comfortable in the kitchen, a master of her skillet, and she was mine.

⤙ CARING FOR CAST IRON ⤚

All of the cast iron that Lodge sells (not including their enameled line, of course) is preseasoned at the foundry, using vegetable oil. As a result, seasoning the pan, the traditional first step in cast iron cookware ownership, is now not necessary. But your preseasoned cookware still benefits from correct care.

HERE'S HOW TO DO IT:

1. Rinse your cast iron cookware with hot water. If there is any stuck-on food, use a stiff brush to remove it. Do not use soap, as any type of detergent will break down the oil-based seasoning.

2. After rinsing, dry the cookware immediately inside and out. If water remains on the surface, rusting can occur, even with a seasoned piece.

3. While the piece is still warm from being washed, use cooking spray or a paper towel soaked with melted vegetable shortening to give the interior and exterior surfaces of the pan (including the underside of the lid if the piece has one) a light coating of oil.

4. Store in a cool, dry place. If the piece has a lid, folded paper towels should be placed between the lid and pot to allow air to circulate.

⤙ WHEN YOU NEED TO RE-SEASON A PAN ⤚

It happens sometimes—a friend helpfully puts your cast iron skillet in the dishwasher without your knowing it or takes a steel scrubbing pad to it, stripping the seasoning from its surface, or you inherit or acquire an older piece of cast iron that needs refurbishing.

HERE'S HOW TO DO IT:

1. Preheat the oven to 350°F. If you have three racks in the oven, remove one and move the others so they are in the two lowest positions.

2. Prepare the piece for re-seasoning by washing it in hot, soapy water, using a stiff brush to remove any stuck-on food. If the pan has surface rust, remove it using fine steel wool or an abrasive soap pad such as Brillo® or S.O.S.® (If a piece is severely rusted, you'll need to take it to a local machine shop to have it sandblasted. It will then need to be re-seasoned IMMEDIATELY.) Rinse and towel-dry the pan immediately and thoroughly.

3. Coat the piece with oil as instructed in Step 3 above, making sure to also include the handle.

4. Place a large sheet of aluminum foil on the lowest oven rack. Set the pan upside down on the rack above it. Bake for 1 hour.

5. If the piece has a lid, set it beside the pan. Close the oven door, turn off the oven, and leave until the pieces cool off. Store as directed above.

❧ METRIC EQUIVALENTS ❧

The recipes that appear in this cookbook use the standard U.S. method for measuring liquid and dry or solid ingredients (teaspoons, tablespoons, and cups). The information on this chart is provided to help cooks outside the United States successfully use these recipes. All equivalents are approximate.

Metric Equivalents for Different Types of Ingredients

A standard cup measure of a dry or solid ingredient will vary in weight depending on the type of ingredient. A standard cup of liquid is the same volume for any type of liquid. Use the following chart when converting standard cup measures to grams (weight) or milliliters (volume).

Standard Cup	Fine Powder (ex. flour)	Grain (ex. rice)	Granular (ex. sugar)	Liquid Solids (ex. butter)	Liquid (ex. milk)
1	140 g	150 g	190 g	200 g	240 ml
¾	105 g	113 g	143 g	150 g	180 ml
⅔	93 g	100 g	125 g	133 g	160 ml
½	70 g	75 g	95 g	100 g	120 ml
⅓	47 g	50 g	63 g	67 g	80 ml
¼	35 g	38 g	48 g	50 g	60 ml
⅛	18 g	19 g	24 g	25 g	30 ml

Useful Equivalents for Dry Ingredients by Weight

(To convert ounces to grams, multiply the number of ounces by 30.)

1 oz	=	¹⁄₁₆ lb	=	30 g
4 oz	=	¼ lb	=	120 g
8 oz	=	½ lb	=	240 g
12 oz	=	¾ lb	=	360 g
16 oz	=	1 lb	=	480 g

Useful Equivalents for Length

(To convert inches to centimeters, multiply the number of inches by 2.5.)

1 in			=	2.5 cm		
6 in	=	½ ft	=	15 cm		
12 in	=	1 ft	=	30 cm		
36 in	=	3 ft	= 1 yd	=	90 cm		
40 in			=	100 cm	=	1 m

Useful Equivalents for Liquid Ingredients by Volume

¼ tsp				=	1 ml
½ tsp				=	2 ml
1 tsp				=	5 ml
3 tsp	=	1 Tbsp		= ½ fl oz	=	15 ml
	2 Tbsp	= ⅛ cup	=	1 fl oz	=	30 ml
	4 Tbsp	= ¼ cup	=	2 fl oz	=	60 ml
	5⅓ Tbsp	= ⅓ cup	=	3 fl oz	=	80 ml
	8 Tbsp	= ½ cup	=	4 fl oz	=	120 ml
	10⅔ Tbsp	= ⅔ cup	=	5 fl oz	=	160 ml
	12 Tbsp	= ¾ cup	=	6 fl oz	=	180 ml
	16 Tbsp	= 1 cup	=	8 fl oz	=	240 ml
	1 pt	= 2 cups	=	16 fl oz	=	480 ml
	1 qt	= 4 cups	=	32 fl oz	=	960 ml
				33 fl oz	=	1000 ml = 1 l

Useful Equivalents for Cooking/Oven Temperatures

	Fahrenheit	Celsius	Gas Mark
Freeze water	32° F	0° C	
Room temperature	68° F	20° C	
Boil water	212° F	100° C	
Bake	325° F	160° C	3
	350° F	180° C	4
	375° F	190° C	5
	400° F	200° C	6
	425° F	220° C	7
	450° F	230° C	8
Broil			Grill

INDEX